Our Story, Saint John's Episcopal Church

Park Slope, Brooklyn

Father C. H. Powers

139 St Johns Place
Brooklyn, NY 11217
www.saintjohnsbrooklyn.com
Email: officesaintjohns@gmail.com

Saint John's Episcopal Church
139 St Johns Place
Brooklyn, New York 11217
www.saintjohnsbrooklyn.com
Email: officesaintjohns@gmail.com

Dedication

This book is dedicated to the memory of all those who have loved God and served God's people from this holy place. May God continue to bless the ministry of such people here in the years to come.

Acknowledgements

Many people have helped me to tell this story and I can't name them all here, but without their help our story would not have been told at all. A few of them include:

Father Joe O'Steen, an old and valued friend helped me a great deal in the early days of this work. He is actively retired after 50 years of priesthood. Having served the church for many years here in the Diocese of Long Island, Father Joe now serves part time at St. Andrew's Episcopal Church in Pearland, Texas where he lives with his sister. He returns to New York twice each year to help me at Saint John's and during several of those recent visits he has researched old vestry minutes and letters, calling out in joy when he found something of interest. It was great fun working with him!

Dr. Juliet Emanuel-George was also an invaluable research assistant on this project. She made several trips to the Brooklyn Historical Society and gleaned several interesting anecdotes which helped to bring some of the characters of our story to life.

Cryder Bankes voluntarily took on the job of parish archivist without the benefit of salary or title as we worked together to sort and then to preserve our historic books, photos and letters. **James Olszewski** helped scan photos and our parish vestry and leadership have been fantastic in providing me some valuable days off to work on this book. The members of the vestry at Saint John's have been incredibly supportive all the time I have been working on this volume. They are a wonderful team and without their support I would not have been able to take the time off other duties to pull all of this together.

Paul Bernstein and his wife **Caryn Benjamin** took some of the wonderful pictures included in this work. Professional photographers, they freely offered their talent to us as good neighbors. I can't thank them enough! Take a look at their work at www.PaulBernstein.Com and www.CarynBenjaminimages.Com.

Finally I want to thank Susan Maldovan, a member of our parish who is also our volunteer Parish Gardner. Susan works professionally in publishing and spent a great deal of time copy editing this work. When I say a great deal of time I mean it! Writing flows fairly easily for me as long as I don't take a lot of time to worry much about structure and spelling, so I don't. That means I relied a great deal on Susan and I cannot thank her enough!

Contents

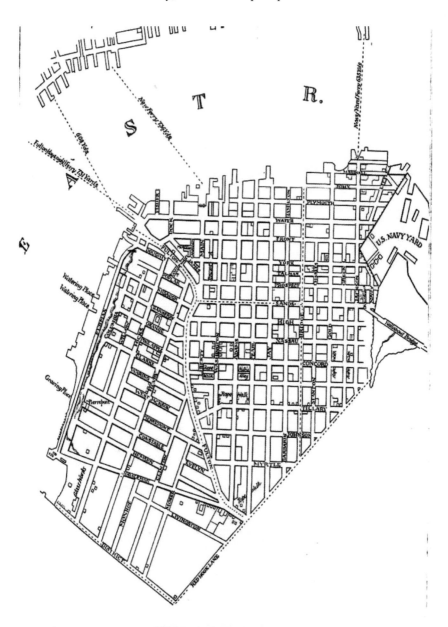

BROOKLYN VILLAGE IN 1827

Redrawn from William Hooker's New Pocket Plan. Courtesy of
the Long Island Historical Society

Preface

As a sort of preface to his Gospel, Saint Luke addressed "Theophilus", perhaps an individual known to Luke or more likely a reference to anyone who is seeking God or information about God saying,

"Inasmuch as many have undertaken to compile a narrative of the things which have been accomplished among us, just as they were delivered to us by those who from the beginning were eyewitnesses and ministers of the word, it seemed good to me also, having followed all things closely for some time past, to write an orderly account for you, most excellent Theophilus, that you may know the truth concerning the things of which you have been informed."

I think this is a good description of what I have tried to do in this book since I have also tried to present an orderly account *"of the things which have been accomplished among us"* in this parish over the past 186 or so years. So I like to think that Luke was my guide in the construction of this work.

Just as Luke made use of Mark's earlier Gospel as a foundation for his own work, I have made extensive use of the History Book compiled in 1975 by Father Clifford Buck and members of the parish. In places I have corrected that text by making use of the wider variety of resources for research available today that was not even dreamed of by my predecessors. Like Luke, I have also found some other information not mentioned in the earlier work which I have added. And, of course, I have added several chapters at the end of the book to bring it all up to the present day.

Most parish histories consist of a list of Rectors and the dates of their service. While such lists are a helpful tool in recounting the chronology of events in parishes, it should be noted that Rectors are not the only ministers in parishes. According to the Book of Common Prayer, the ministers of the church are *"lay persons, bishops, priests, and deacons."*

> *The ministry of lay persons is to represent Christ and his Church; to bear witness to him wherever they may be; and, according to the gifts given them, to carry on Christ's work of reconciliation in the world; and to take their place in the life, worship, and governance of the Church.*
>
> *The ministry of a priest is to represent Christ and his Church, particularly as pastor to the people; to share with the bishop in the overseeing of the Church; to proclaim the Gospel; to administer the sacraments; and to bless and declare pardon in the name of God.*

Rectors are important officials in parishes and they usually set the liturgical tone of worship and have great influence in the direction of life and service found in parishes. But they are not the parish and parish history books should not be primarily about them, but about the parish and the people they have ministered to and with.

Having said that, I should point out that the materials available for compiling parish histories are very limited by the very nature of the institution we are writing about. Parishes are living, breathing entities where life takes place in the moment just as it does for individual people. Sermons are given each week, but in most parishes are usually not recorded.

Evangelism and outreach take place constantly, but few records are kept of what was done. Visitation of the sick, fellowship, education and lots of other things go on all the time, but few written records reflect their impact upon individuals or the wider community.

Since vestry minutes are required by both church canon and state laws governing religious corporations, they are the most readily available historical sources for writing a Parish history. Unfortunately, vestry minutes usually consist of little more than what is required of them by law. So they usually make very dry reading of the passage of resolutions regarding the expense of funds and various administrative matters. Great and traumatic sociological upheavals can be occurring all around the parish and the world in which it lives without being much noted in the minutes of any vestry. It is not that vestries are unconcerned with current affairs but that they are not the focus of their attention during meetings.

In recent times the Internet has provided some wonderful new tools for researchers. In many places local newspapers and magazines have been digitalized and placed online so they can be searched rather easily from the comfort of the church office. Here in Brooklyn the public library has digitalized the local newspaper which was called the ***Brooklyn Daily Eagle*** from the early 1841 through 1902. The Brooklyn Historical Society has also digitalized much of its collection and made it available to the public. This has been a tremendous help as I and others have conducted research for this current volume. But even with the help of these new resources, so much of the life which filled this parish is still a mystery since even the names of so many of the laity who taught Sunday School, cooked and served dinners, prepared the Altar for services, comforted the sick and performed so many other acts of kindness and ministry are lost in the mists of time.

A few years ago I attended a series of Lenten Lectures in Brooklyn offered by Father John Farrell on Celtic Spirituality. I learned that the ancient Celts felt that there was only a sort of thin membrane dividing this time from all that had gone before. They felt that sometimes, in some places, if you were very still and very quiet you could perhaps almost see images of those who have lived before, perhaps just vaguely out of the corner of your eye. I have often thought of that when I have been inside Saint John's Church early in the morning or at twilight. As the dim light filters through the windows I can almost see the thousands of people who have lived, shared, cried and laughed in this holy place as they have worshiped together at masses, weddings, funerals, baptisms, and so much more. It is their faith and their contributions, which have built this holy place, that I have tried to present in this work. I am very grateful to them and to those who helped me in recent months, as well as to Father Clifford Buck, the Brooklyn Public Library and the Brooklyn Historical Society, without which this volume would not have been possible. I hope that you have as much fun reading it as I had writing it!

Father Clarence (Clark) H. Powers,
      Sixteenth Rector of Saint John's Church

Father Powers

The original wooden building on Johns Street as it appeared after the bell tower was added in 1861

CHAPTER ONE: LAYING THE FOUNDATIONS

Our first parish history book begins by saying that the Dutch were the first settlers of "the hinterland of New Amsterdam" which later became Brooklyn and that they purchased the land it was built on from the Montauk Indians. That is not exactly true. There were actually a large number of Native Americans living on the long island near New Amsterdam, a small port city on the tip of Manhattan Island, that was the center of the Dutch colony of New Netherlands. The Dutch had inhabited that region since the 1630's.

What later became Brooklyn was originally inhabited by a group who called themselves the Lenape, which means "the People." They included the Nayack and the Canarsee, who planted corn and tobacco and fished in the rivers. The Dutch called these Native Americans "river Indians" or "wild people" and the land they inhabited *"Breuckelen"* (broken land).

Between the 1630's and the 1680's, European settlers purchased land from Native American tribes throughout present-day Brooklyn. But the purchases were not always peaceful achieved. Violent skirmishes over contested lands pitted Dutch settlers against native tribes – and competing tribes against each other – throughout the seventeenth century. Some Native Americans were taken as slaves and sold off to Dutch outposts in the Caribbean. Regular smallpox outbreaks further decimated the Canarsee population. By the 1680's, the Dutch had bought all of Kings County but by then most of the native inhabitants were dead or enslaved. By the beginning of the eighteenth century most remaining Native Americans had migrated further east on Long Island, or moved westward into the Delaware River valley and beyond.[1]

The Dutch founded five villages in the area now called Brooklyn: Bushwick, Brooklyn, Flatbush (originally known as Midwout), Flatlands, and New Utrecht. Gravesend, a sixth village, was founded in 1643 by Lady Deborah Moody, an Englishwoman who was fleeing religious persecution

---

[1] *Actually, the Montaukett Indians lived much further east on the island.* http://www.brooklynhistory.org/exhibitions/lefferts/brooklyns-dutch-frontier/

in England and the Massachusetts Bay Colony. The British captured the Dutch territory in 1674, and gathered the six villages into Kings County, part of the crown colony of New York.

A census taken in 1698 counted 2,017 people in Kings County. About half of these early settlers were Dutch. The others came from Germany, England, France, and Scandinavia, and included a large number of black slaves brought from Africa.

Slavery flourished in these rich farmlands during the 18th century. By 1771, just before the Revolutionary War, slaves represented nearly one third of the population of Kings County, an important factor in the early life of Saint John's Church.

During the Revolution, British troops nearly destroyed George Washington's inexperienced Army at the battle of Brooklyn in 1776. The fighting ranged from Gravesend to Gowanus, and the Colonial Army narrowly escaped annihilation by slipping across the East River to Manhattan during a foggy night. The British then occupied Manhattan and Brooklyn for the duration of the war.[2]

After it had recovered from ravages of the war, Brooklyn was officially incorporated as a village in 1816, and was incorporated as the City of Brooklyn in 1834. By 1826 Brooklyn Village had less than 10,000 inhabitants of diverse backgrounds and races.

King George IV, eldest son of the George III, was on the throne of England. King Charles X, youngest brother of Louis XVI, who actively supported our Revolution with men, money and arms, was reigning in France. John Quincy Adams was the sixth president of the United States. His father, John Adams, the second president, and Thomas Jefferson, the third president, both died on Independence Day, July 4, 1826. There were no telegraph lines, telephones, automobiles, radios or even express trains in those days, so that it was several days later that the news of the deaths of these two national heroes reached Brooklyn, where workmen were building the first Saint John's Church.

The origin of the church is unique in that it was planned, erected and paid for by the Reverend Evan Malbone Johnson, who became the first Rector. He operated it at his own expense until it was purchased by the congregation in 1832 and served without pay for the first 20 years![3]

---

[2] http://www.thirteen.org/brooklyn/history/history2.html

[3] *And this not because he was rich. The property which came to his care, had to be improved by building and other loans, which required large realizations to pay the interest, and nothing but great attention and good management could have kept it from becoming submerged by taxes and assessments, in the advancing progress of Brooklyn.*

Born on June 6, 1792, in Newport, Rhode Island, he obtained a classical education at college in Rhode Island and at Cambridge, Massachusetts, where he became a candidate for Holy Orders. He was ordained at Trinity Church, Newport, by Bishop Alexander V. Griswold on July 8, 1813.

Shortly afterwards he was invited to New York City to serve as curate at the fashionable Grace Church and later became Rector of Saint James Church in Newtown, Long Island.[4]

There he married Maria L. Johnson[5] of New York in 1814 with whom he had one son. After her death in 1825, he married Maria Purdy of Newtown, with whom he had three children.

In Newtown he acquired a farm that he managed in addition to his duties in the church. After some years he determined to sell the farm and to use the funds to build a new church. By 1826 he had sold it for $4000, a great sum in those days, and moved to Brooklyn where he purchased another farm on the outskirts of the village.

It was there that he built the first Saint John's Church on a corner of that farm which later became the corner of Johnson and Washington Streets, which today is directly across the street from the Brooklyn Central Post Office. Saint John's became the second parish in Brooklyn, the first being Saint Ann's, which was founded in 1784 and has come to be called the "mother" church of Episcopalian Brooklyn.

In a sermon preached on the occasion of the 100th Anniversary of the Parish, historian Fred Clarke said of those bygone days:

> *"Saint Ann's Church, which was organized in 1784, was on Sands Street, having been named for Ann Sands (not Saint Anne, mother of the Blessed Virgin, as might be supposed), who*

---

http://www.panix.com/~cassidy/STILES/EPISCOPALCHURCHES.html#NOTE11

[4] *Saint James Church was founded in 1704 and officially chartered in 1761 by King George III. It was the first parish in Elmhurst, called Newtown in colonial times. One of Saint James' earliest Rectors, the Reverend Dr. Samuel Seabury Jr., was consecrated in 1784 at Aberdeen, Scotland, by bishops of the Scottish Episcopal Church to be the first bishop of the Episcopal Church. Ironically, this parish, once served by the radically inclusive Father Johnson, voted to leave the Episcopal Church in 2005 over the inclusion of gay people. Since then the parish property was returned by Court Action to the Diocese of Long Island. LONG ISLAND: Court rules for diocese, wider church in property case, by Mary Frances Schjonberg, ENS March 26, 2008 http://www.episcopalchurch.org/81803_95981_ENG_HTM.htm*

[5] *obviously a popular name as we will see later*

Saint Ann's Church on Sands Street about 1824

was largely instrumental in its founding. Sands Street was a very fashionable street in those days and my own grandmother told me how much the New York girls valued the chance of walking along Sands Street Sunday afternoons with a naval midshipman."

In the original 1826 Parish Register Father Johnson vividly describes the early days of Saint John's in somewhat archaic language:

"In consequence of the increasing growth of the Village of Brooklyn, the design of building a new Episcopal Church was formed by Evan Malbone Johnson in the spring of A.D. 1826. In the course of that summer, he caused a plain, wooden building to be erected at the corner of Washington and Johnson Streets, said building is fifty feet by fifty. It was first opened by him for Divine Service on Sunday the 24th of September 1826. The pulpit was supplied by him and the Reverend John A. Hicks, alternately, during the winter. In March Doctor Johnson removed from New York, where he had been settled twelve years, to Brooklyn. I took sole charge of the congregation."

Holy Communion was first administered on April 15, 1827, Easter Day, to nineteen communicants and, though slavery was not abolished in New York State until July 4, 1827, it is interesting to note that several of these people were listed as "colored". This is not surprising since Father Johnson[6] later became a well-known opponent of slavery in New York State and the nation. In a letter he wrote to the Convention of the Diocese of New

---

[6] *The title "Father", which is commonly used today in the Episcopal Church, probably would not have been one adopted by the Reverend Johnson in his day. However, it suits the taste of this editor and will be used wherever appropriate throughout this work with the caveat that it is a modern redaction.*

York in 1844 concerning the admission of Saint Phillip's Church, a black parish, as a full member of the Diocese he said:

> *"I have been brought truly to believe that God hath made of one blood" the whole race of man. I think the more we can realize the great truths, that every member of the Catholic Church is also a member of the body of Christ –and that in him we are all one – the more shall we disregard the wicked notion, that the colour of the skin ought to make any difference whatever in our intercourse, as Christians, with those who, with us, are buried "with him by baptism in his death.* [7]

Influenced by its abolitionist founder, Saint John's was a multiracial place of worship from its foundation, and though it has undergone many changes throughout its long history, it is still so today.

The Church was consecrated by the Right Reverend Bishop Hobart on the 10th day of July, 1827, and called Saint John's Church.[8] The congregation was incorporated by election on Easter Monday, April 16, 1827.[9]

The Original Cornerstone

The cornerstone was actually laid on May 9, 1827 and bears the following inscription: [7]

"Saint John's Church was erected by Evan Malbone Johnson, AD. 1826, the cornerstone of which was laid by the Masonic Fraternity on the 9th day of May, John Henry Hobart then being Bishop of the Diocese."

Faith In Their Own Color, *Craig D Townsend, Columbia University Press 2005, page 109 – 110*

[8] *The church was named by lot, at the time of laying the cornerstone, which was done," says Mr. Johnson's manuscripts, " without any Previous conference with any of the inhabitants, for fear of exciting the jealousy of the members of the old (Reformed Dutch) church."*

[9] *An excerpt from the Certificate of Incorporation is presented: "Recorded March 19th 1827, L. Bi, page 13. ... all persons of full age belonging to the Church Congregation or Society at the Village of Brooklyn in the County of Kings... met at said church for the*

First Dutch Reformed Church
of Brooklyn, 1666

It was removed in October of 1869 when the old building was sold, but it is not certain where it was stored until the church was expanded in 1889, when it was then placed just inside the new entrance where it may still be seen today, although it is in a serious state of deterioration.

Brooklyn in those days was still heavily influenced by its large Dutch population, most of whom were members of the Dutch Reformed Church. The First Dutch Reformed Church of Brooklyn, now known as Old First Church, on Seventh Avenue in Park Slope, was in the 19th century situated in the middle of Fulton Road, near current Borough Hall. Oddly enough, these two churches that were so physically close together in another part of Brooklyn in the 19th century, find themselves in a similar geographical position in the Park Slope of today. They were also close in a familial sense since Evan Johnson's wife was the granddaughter of a pastor of that church whose name interestingly enough was also Johnson, though no apparent relationship to our own first Rector. Her father had also been a Dutch Pastor who had died of consumption when she was a child. She was raised by her maternal grandfather, Peter Roosevelt of Jamaica, Queens, who was an Episcopalian.

Married into a Dutch clergy family, Father Johnson seems to have been so popular among them that he was often called "***Domine***" by them and others in Brooklyn, an affectionate term for Dutch ministers. In addition to his work as Rector of Saint John's Church, he took a keen interest in all community activities. In particular, he was a leader in the cause of the "common" school (today we would call it a public school), which was opposed by many wealthy residents. Education by a governess or tutor, or at private "finishing" schools was the order of the day for those who could afford it. Father Johnson became Chairman of the Citizen's

---

*purpose of incorporating themselves under the act entitled: **An Act to provide for the Incorporation of Religious Societies'** and the act to annul same. Monday in the week called Easter Week was in like manner fixed on as the day on which the said offices of Church Wardens and Vestrymen shall annually hereafter cease and their successors in office be chosen and the name or title of 'The Rector, Church Wardens and Vestrymen of Saint John's Church at Brooklyn' was in like manner fixed on and agreed to as that by which the said Church Congregation or Society shall be known in law."*

Committee which was formed to create and then expand public education in Brooklyn. Religious education was also very important to him and he was active in the organization of the Brooklyn Sunday School Union which was launched at the Apprentices' Library by representatives of the Presbyterian, Baptist, Reformed Dutch and Saint John's churches, an early example of ecumenical cooperation.[10]

He also helped to found the Long Island Bible Society and served as chaplain in the Grand Masonic Lodge. A publication describing Brooklyn Village of the day records that Saint John's Sunday School owned the biggest library in the village, and that the church officers made it available to the public. By 1832 this library contained 400 volumes – an amazing collection of books in those days. It later was donated to the public to form the nucleus of the present Brooklyn Public Library system.

At one of the first vestry meetings held on March 2, 1827, the vestry voted to

"accept proposals of the Reverend Mister Johnson for the purchase of the church and grounds,"

although this was not done until 1832. Pew purchase prices were set from $30 to $200, depending on location, and corresponding quarterly rents from $1.00 to $5.00. In 1843 Father Johnson sent an important message to the vestry about seating in the church:

"I would wish the vestry to remember that it is the glory of the gospel of Christ that it is to be preached to the poor - and that the Church extends her arms to embrace as well the low as the high, the poor as the rich, the servant as the master. How can all such enjoy the blessings offered to them by the Church if by any arrangement a portion of these classes be excluded from the place where is offered up the Holy Sacrifice? My object in sending you this communication is, to recommend that you take such order and give it publicity, that no person whatsoever of any description shall ever apply at our Church and not be supplied with a seat

---

[10] *This Sunday School Union grew steadily and mightily and reached such proportions that eventually all public schools in Brooklyn were closed on a Thursday in June for its annual parade. The event was marked by thousands of children with flags, banners and a few "Episcopal processional crosses" marching from Flatbush Avenue around the plaza, past reviewing stands in front of the magnificent Grand Army Arch, and into Prospect Park. It was there that church, school and city officials (almost always the mayor) made tributes and presented various awards to the participating groups. Like so many civic traditions and celebrations, this one too has been relegated to the annals of history and memory.*

(gratuitously, if necessary), as long as we have any room. I would have the sexton instructed to remain at the door until after the second lesson, and to show to a seat every person who makes application for one."

It is not known at what date pews became rent-free and open to all, but this was a first step in that direction.[11] Nonetheless, pew rentals provided for the operating expenses of the church for many more years. Luckily, these expenses were moderate even in the early 19th century. In 1827, as we have noted above, the Rector worked for free, the sexton received $40.00 per annum, the entire church was painted for the sum of $7.45 and the next year the collection at Easter was $3.00, at Whitsunday $3.31, and at Christmas $3.60!

In the 20 years that Father Johnson served as Rector of Saint John's Church, he baptized a total of 1346 people. That's an average of 67.3 persons per year! According to his records he also married 587 couples during that time. He listed 499 total communicants for the parish in those years according to a sermon he delivered at Saint John's Church on October 14, 1861, at an evening service celebrating the opening of the renovated wooden building on Johnson Street.[12]

After 20 years of faithful service Father Evan M. Johnson retired in July of 1847. He had literally built the church himself and then helped it grow in membership, strength and involvement in the larger life of the Diocese and the Episcopal Church. He was beloved not only among his parishioners but also in the wider Brooklyn community and throughout the Diocese and the state of New York for his pastoral care and leadership.

A few weeks after his resignation he went back to doing what he did best, building churches – as he formed another congregation in a room on Jackson Street, which became Saint Michael's Church.[13] He continued

---

[11] *Father E. M. Johnson felt so strongly about abolishing pew rentals that upon leaving Saint John's Church in 1847 he founded Saint Michael's "Free" Episcopal Church. The "Free" refers to the fact that pews were not rented or sold. The church was funded by "subscription", what we call pledges today.*

[12] *See End Notes*

[13] *St. Michael's Church. In the year 1847, the Rev. Evan M. Johnson resigned the rectorship of St. John's church, Brooklyn, for the purpose of establishing a new congregation in the fifth ward of the city, at that time lamentably deficient in religious privileges, there being but one house of worship within its limits, and a population of twenty or thirty thousand souls. Hiring a lecture room in Marshall street, near the Jackson ferry, he commenced to hold meetings in September of that year.*
Such was the success which attended the labors of the Rev. gentleman, that this

his ministry of planting churches, caring for the poor and remaining vocally opposed to slavery for almost 20 years in Brooklyn and New York City as is attested by the following notation from minutes of Saint John's Church vestry shortly after his death in March of 1865:

> *At a meeting held in the Chapel after service the Committee on Resolutions presented the following:*

> *The Reverend Evan Malbone Johnson, late Rector of Saint Michael's Church in this city and the founder and for many years the Rector of Saint John's Church at Brooklyn having been removed from the scene of his earthly labors, a meeting of the Rector, Wardens, and Vestrymen of Saint John's Church was held on Monday evening, March 20, when the following resolutions were unanimously adopted:*

> *Resolved. That while bowing with humble submission to this afflictive dispensation of Divine Providence we recognize in the decease of this venerable and devoted servant of God the loss to our city of one of its oldest, most useful, and respected citizens; to the poor a true, liberal, and faithful friend, and to the church of a zealous, faithful, and efficient laborer for the salvation of souls and an earnest defender of the Faith once delivered to the Saints. His venerable form, and quaint, frank, truthful, and outspoken utterances, will long be remembered by all who knew him.*

> *Resolved, that as individuals and as a vestry we present to the bereaved family of our departed Brother in Christ the expression of our warmest sympathies and condolences in their affliction, with the earnest prayer that divine grace and consolation be abundantly theirs.*

---

building soon became insufficient to accommodate the congregation, and he accordingly leased from the city for ten years, the building known as the Eastern Market, in High street, in the Fifth ward. Services were first held here on the 5th of February, 1848. Soon this building failed to accommodate the constantly increasing congregation, and in 1849, the Rev. Mr. Johnson caused to be built an addition to it, some forty by fifty feet in dimensions, which made a very comfortable and commodious church edifice. In 1852, the Board of Education established a primary week day school, for which the church was used, and where some two hundred children received instruction.
http://www.panix.com/~cassidy/STILES/EPISCOPALCHURCHES.html#STMICHAELS

The Reverend Samuel Johnson
Second Rector

Resolved. That in testimony of regard for the deceased appropriate drapery be put in our church, and remain until the great Festival of Easter.

Resolved. That an attested copy of these resolutions be sent to the family of our deceased Brother, and published in the city papers.[14]

Oddly enough, the second Rector of the parish was also named Johnson. The Reverend Samuel Roosevelt Johnson was no blood relation to the first Rector but was related in law. Brother-in-law of the Reverend Evan Malbone Johnson, he served briefly from 1847 until November 1850. The importance of Saint John's Church in those early days is evidenced by its hosting of a special convention of the Episcopal Diocese of New York,[15] which met in Saint John's "Chapel"[16] to consider certain special amendments to the canons of

---

[14] *Mr. Johnson's good nature and liberal tendencies caused him to be, extensively sought by parties desirous of being united in matrimony, and at the time of his half century discourse, the number of marriages performed by him had reached as high as two thousand. No man's life was more studded with deeds of actual and daily kindness than the domine's, as he was generally called throughout the city. He would at any time rise at midnight or daylight to marry the humblest couple or do the smallest deed of kindness. During the whole of his life here, none of our clergymen was ever half so much seen among the people as the domine. Almost any day at about ten or eleven o'clock he might be seen turning the corner of Pearl street from the north Into Myrtle avenue; for he lived where his ancient farm house stood, and in walking through Pearl street follows in some degree the ancient cow path of his farm. His style of dress was plain, simple and old fashioned, a felt hat, always carelessly crumpled ground the rim, surmounted the face of an ancient Roman, crowned with a strong crop of standing hair, as white as snow; and an atmosphere of ease and benignity surrounded him, inviting everybody to stop and have a chat with him. He might have been, and indeed frequently was, taken for one of the ancient crop of Dutchmen, an error which his name assisted in producing ; but, as we have seen, the nearest he came to it was in marrying into a Dutch family. http://www.panix.com/~cassidy/STILES/EPISCOPALCHURCHES.html#NOTE15*

[15] *The Diocese of Long Island had not yet been created.*

[16] *"Chapel" rather than "Church" is often found in various historical references. The use of this term may well imply that whatever building is currently being referred to is not the final, larger structure that is imagined.*

the diocese. Elected Professor of Systematic Divinity at General Theological Seminary, Dr. Johnson resigned as Rector in November of 1850 but continued to be actively involved in the parish ministry, at least in a part-time manner, for the next few years.

There is some confusion regarding the third Rector of Saint John's Church, the Reverend N. A. Okeson, which is reflected in the parish history published in 1976. That book reports that *"parish records contain a curious letter from the Reverend N. A. Okeson addressed to the wardens and vestry of Saint John's Church accepting their call to become their Rector dated December 10, 1850."*

That letter is still in our parish archives. The first book goes on to say,

> *There are equally mysterious references to a Reverend D. V. M. Johnson (another Johnson relative?) who apparently took some services during 1852. There are no further records of, or references to, either of them, nor are they to be found in the archives of the diocese.*

More modern research on the Internet indicates that The Reverend D. V. M. Johnson was the founder of Trinity Episcopal Church, which was the foundation from which Saint Luke's Church was born. (Which later merged with Saint Matthew's to form what is known today as Saint Luke and Saint Matthew's Church) He also founded Saint Mary's Church on what is now Classon Avenue[17] and apparently helped out at Saint John's.

---

[17] *In March, 1835, Trinity Episcopal Church was organized and a stone edifice erected during the same year on Clinton avenue, between Atlantic avenue and Fulton street, which location was in what was then known as the Wallabout district. Rev. D. V. M. JOHNSON was the first rector and continued for a year. In 1841 the parish became embarrassed and the church was sold, but was purchased and services revived by the present St. Luke's congregation in 1842.*

St. Mary's Church was begun on Classon avenue at the Wallabout, by the Rev. D. V. M. Johnson, while in charge of Trinity church. A Sunday School was commenced in March, 1836, and formed the nucleus of a church. Here the Rev. Mr. Johnson held services on Sunday afternoons for about six months. In May, 1837, Mr. Joseph Hunter took charge of the school, and served as a lay-reader to a small congregation which assembled with the children. During the year an edifice of a very limited extent was erected, and a church organized, to which the name of St. Mary's was given. This was consecrated on the first of February, 1840, and was enlarged in 1841, so as to accommodate about two hundred and fifty persons.
http://www.panix.com/~cassidy/STILES/EPISCOPALCHURCHES.html

An examination of the vestry minutes of 1852 – 1853 clearly shows that the Reverend N. A. Okeson was present as Rector in January 1851 and that he presided over all meetings of the vestry during that period. His name is also to be found in editions of the Brooklyn Daily Eagle newspaper and in other historical sources.[18]

The vestry minutes state that his resignation was accepted on October 20, 1852. Why he resigned after such a relatively short period of time is not part of the record, but this in itself is not unusual. A few other Rectors stayed even less time and some have left without giving reasons for their resignation.[19] So it is rather curious that this Rector was left out of our history and such a great point was made in the first book to explain why parish records differ from diocesan records in terms of the numbers of Rectors who had served Saint John's Church.

Perhaps some of the confusion as to the status of this Rector is due to the circumstances under which he resigned. This presents yet another minor mystery. In May of 1852 vestry records indicate that a special

---

[18] *In fact he seems to have had quite an active ministry while here. An article in the Brooklyn Daily Eagle newspaper of April 12, 1852, describes a service of Confirmation held at Saint John's Church in which 70 – 80 people were Confirmed and which lists the Rector as the Reverend N. A. Okeson. The article describes this number as the largest class ever confirmed at Saint John's Church! A great deal of ministry was going on at that time presumably by, and under the direction of Father Okeson the Rector.*

[19] *One was especially tight lipped about why he was resigning - I love it. Brooklyn Daily Eagle Oct 9, 1902; Section:None; Page Number:20 reports*
The Rev. Dr. George F. Breed, whose resignation as rector of St. John's Episcopal Church was announced in yesterday's Eagle, declines to state his reasons for resigning.
These reasons are his own affair, he says.
The members of the vestry who received his resignation at a vestry meeting Tuesday night say that what transpired at that meeting was confidential and they are mystified over the publication of his resignation.
"My reasons for resigning are my own affair," said Dr. Breed this morning. I've got no statement whatever to make."
"Is it true that you intend to go abroad for a year?" the reporter asked.
"You can publish that if you want to," was his reply. "That's what I told the other reporters who came here. The newspapers don't publish the facts, even when they can get them. A paper distorted an interview with my wife yesterday."
"Well, is it true that you resigned to go abroad?" the reporter asked.
"I don't know whether I am going abroad or not. What right has anybody got to demand that I make up my mind in fifteen minutes as to what I am going to do?"
When told that it was a common thing for rectors resigning a charge to announce their reason for doing so, Dr. Breed replied:
"Well, that's not my way."

committee was formed to investigate some particular financial matter which is not disclosed. That committee reported its findings to the vestry on October 20, 1852, and it was at that meeting that the resignation of the Rector was received. The committee report is not included in the minutes.[20] No further information regarding that report or the reasons for Father Okeson's resignation have been found.

On the surface it would seem that the two things are connected, reflecting rather poorly on the character of the Rector. But one

The Reverend Thomas F. Guion
Fourth Rector

should be careful in drawing such conclusions against the character of someone long dead who has no ability to defend himself. Although nothing more is reported in the records of Saint John's Church, research of Episcopal Church sources and newspaper articles in indicate that he returned to his native state of Virginia to accept the call of Rector at St. Paul's Church, Norfolk, where remained for many years with no apparent hint of scandal.

Conspiracy theorists might have a field day addressing the question of why this third Rector of the parish might have been intentionally left out of our history book! It is hard to see how such a mistake could have been unintentionally made in the light of both vestry minutes and newspaper accounts which show his presence in office as Rector. So it is a bit of a mystery and, like so many others in history, will probably remain so. But at least we can set the record straight in this second edition of our parish history and reclaim Father Okeson as one of our own.

Whatever may have happened, it would seem that our parish records must be adjusted as a result of this new finding. Our list of Rectors from the beginning until the present day should include 16 names rather than the currently accepted 15. Therefore, the current holder of this office, the Reverend Clarence H. Powers is the 16th Rector of Saint John's, not the 15th as he has always thought!

---

[20] *I would love to see the report of that special financial committee! But this will probably never happen. Perhaps those who take minutes for parish organizations and vestries should take note that important events such as this should be more carefully documented to avoid confusing future generations!*

The Reverend Thomas F. Guion was instituted as the fourth Rector in 1853. He became a beloved pastor and well-known figure in the Brooklyn of his day. He also seemed to have been what we sometimes call a **"brick-and-mortar"** sort of priest. After a few years in office, the old wooden church building was closed for awhile as it was repaired, enlarged, and renovated as we have already noted above. Services were conducted during this renovation in space rented at the nearby Packer Institute.

A report from the committee on Carpet and Cushions to the vestry in September of 1861 describes the carpet which was to be laid down and says that the cushions are to be *"of the Best quality stuff with Purified hogshair at $.50 per running foot."*

At the same meeting it was decided to move paintings formerly in the church on either side of the chancel, to the **Sunday School Room**. What those paintings depicted and where that room might have been located is somewhat of a mystery since later in the meeting it was resolved to sell the Sunday School building (wherever that was) and have it removed from the property. It is possible that this building housed the Brooklyn Sunday School Union, of which Saint John's was an active member, and not just the parish Sunday School, but more research will need to be done to determine if this was the case.

The renovations were completed in time for Saint John's Church to host a special convention of the diocese of New York later in the year. To mark the reopening of the church, a special service is described in the Brooklyn Daily Eagle of October 14, 1861:

> *"The old 'Church in the Meadows' endeared to us by so many pleasant associations and ... memories was re-opened yesterday by the memorable Bishop Potter, in the presence of a full congregation. Just before the sermon, the Pastor, Mr. Guion, in brief and appropriate words, welcomed his parishioners back to, their old homestead."[21]*

It is interesting to note that even as the renovation was taking place and more than a full year before the reopening of the renovated church, the vestry formed a committee in May of 1860 to look into the sale of the property and to search for a new location! This probably indicates that there was a bit of disagreement within the vestry and parish about its future. Discussion of this issue continued and intensified over the next few years, resulting ultimately in the relocation of the parish to what is now Park Slope.

---

[21] *See End Note for a full copy of the sermon from the first Rector.*

But before this was sorted out Father Guion died in 1862 and was buried in Greenwood Cemetery.

The high regard in which he was held by members of the parish is attested by a beautiful large memorial window in his memory that was installed a few years later behind the High Altar of the new church building in Park Slope. That window is now behind the choir.

Vestry minutes of October 26, 1862, include a touching memorial, which says

Guion Memorial Window, now above and partially obscured by the Choir loft.

"during the whole period of his ministry, his entire strength and energies were devoted to the welfare of this parish, raising it from the state of depression in which it then existed, to that of comparative prosperity, that it now enjoys."

Anytime a beloved Rector leaves a parish, some degree of mourning takes place, especially when a beloved Rector dies in office; as your editor can attest having become Rector himself shortly after the death in office of Father Clifford Buck in 1985.

A period of administrative turmoil often follows such a death and certainly seems to have been the case after the death of Father Guion. Vestry minutes for several months described the call of one clergyman after another to become Rector, all of whom declined. On January 30, 1863, the vestry addressed a letter to the congregation saying that they were unable to agree upon a candidate for Rector. They therefore deferred this decision until after a new vestry was elected and in place.

The confusion and disagreement in parish leadership is reflected by numerous resignations of vestry members and many occasions where vestry meetings could not be held due to the lack of a quorum. Finally the new vestry invited the Reverend George F. Seymour[22] to become Rector and he

---

[22] *born in New York on January 5, 1829, he studied at General Theological Seminary and was ordained deacon on December 17, 1854, and priest on September 23, 1855, by Bishop Horatio Potter, of New York. He served a parish in Dutchess county, New York, where he founded and became the first warden of Saint Stephen's College. In 1861 he accepted the Rectorship of Saint*

Bishop Horatio Potter

The Reverend George F. Seymour
Fifth Rector

accepted by letter dated June 9, 1863, a copy of which is in our vestry minutes.

At first it seemed as if he might reject the call as well but, at the urgent request of Bishop Horatio Potter, he went, as the bishop expressed it,

"to lead a forlorn hope" in recovering the parish of Saint John's, Brooklyn, New York, from the distressing condition into which internal dissension had brought it.[23]

Not surprisingly his ministry, was not to be an easy one. He remained in office only few months longer than Father Okeson had done and spent most of that time helping the congregation deal with the vacuum of leadership that often results in any organization after the death of a very popular and strong leader. The first few years of the current Rector's ministry, following the death of Father Clifford Buck in 1985, were spent in a similar fashion.

The three years of Father Seymour's ministry at Saint John's were marked by continued turmoil, which included the firing of several members of staff and the resignation of others, including choir masters, choristers and sextons. Rumors were rife in the midst of such confusion in leadership.

Mary's Church, Manhattanville, and in 1862 that of Christ Church, Hudson, New York.

[23] *http://sangamon.ilgenweb.net/1904/seymour.htm*

Minutes of a vestry meeting held on March 13, 1866, include a resolution to be read to the congregation to the effect that the opinions being expressed by some people in the church that the Rector's position was only temporary be corrected! It goes on to request that the Rector change his mind and stay on as their pastor.   Whatever the source of these rumors may have been, there appears to have been some truth in them. In a letter posted from the General Theological Seminary and dated July 11, 1866, Father Seymour wrote,

> *"my mind is clear, gentlemen, that I owe it to my Divine Master, to you, and to the Parishioners of Saint John's, perhaps I should add to myself also, to relinquish the Rectorship to which you called me three years ago. I therefore tender to you, with real sorrow, my resignation as Rector of Saint John's church, Brooklyn, New York – such resignation to take effect on Monday the first day of October next."*

Another letter in our archives dated October 05, 1866, indicates that he has indeed resigned and urges them to *"take speedy action in calling a Rector."* Saying that he does not want to influence them in their choice, he nonetheless goes on to say that

> *" it would grieve me… to have the parish pass into the hands of a lax churchman, of one who would do as certain ill-informed and thoughtless clergyman of the city have done, disregard the terms of their ordination vows, and the moderate reasonable distinctions of their ecclesiastical superior and encourage by their precepts and example lawlessness and disorder."*

He also advises against having candidates for Rector come to preach in what he calls "**a trial**" saying that the effect of

> *"having one and another come to the parish in this way is to demoralize the congregation, to degrade the character of a clergyman in their eyes, and to injure their own souls."*

He encouraged them rather to just call a clergyman of good reputation.

This letter includes a financial report which says that from October 1865 to October 1866 a total of $13,820.77 was contributed to Saint John's – an amount he says far surpassing his expectations. He concludes that the church will soon be out of debt if this degree of giving continues. He then reports that he has baptized 16 adults and five infants, performed 25 marriages and 56 burials, and has presented 53 people for Confirmation. This letter was read at the meeting of the vestry of October 05, 1866, which Father Seymour said he would not attend in order to give the vestrymen a chance to discuss the future of the parish without him being present. Our records indicate that the vestry met on four additional occasions during that month but unfortunately does not give us any information as to what was discussed.

The Reverend Alexander Burgess
Sixth Rector

On November 26 the vestry finally accepted the resignation of Father Seymour. He left the parish to accept the position of Saint Mark's Professor of Ecclesiastical History at the General Theological Seminary and later he became the first Bishop of Springfield, Illinois. As Bishop Potter had hoped, he brought a great deal of pastoral care and administrative expertise to the parish, which was suffering greatly as it mourned his beloved predecessor. Even upon leaving, he influenced the selection of his successor as we have seen in his letter of October 05, 1866, something many priests would love to be able to do!

The Reverend Alexander Burgess was installed as Rector on the Feast of Epiphany 1867. Born in Providence, Rhode Island, on October 31, 1819, he graduated from Brown University in 1838 and from General Theological Seminary in New York in 1841. He was ordained deacon on November 3, 1842, and priest November 1, 1843. He served several parishes in New England before coming to Saint John's in 1867.

The General Theological Seminary of
the Episcopal Church, 1890

Despite Father Seymour's hopeful observations regarding the parish debt, the financial situation seems to have gotten worse. Several loans were taken out to pay bills. Subscriptions (pledges) were requested from members of the parish to pay them, and then new loans were sought. At one meeting the finance committee reports that two persons who were behind in their "subscriptions" were contacted. One paid up and the other did not. A lawyer was hired to sue the one who did not pay!

A house at 20 Johnson Street, owned by the Church, was made available to Father Burgess as a place to live rent-free as part of his compensation, but he was required by the vestry to take responsibility for all repairs and upkeep. [12] They apologized for this unusual requirement but said it was due to dire financial necessity.

Later in the year the parish was assessed $2000 by the new Diocese of Long Island as its portion of the amount needed to support a Bishop. The minutes say that after a careful consideration of the subject the vestry decided that in *view of the present financial condition of the parish* the sum named was too large. A later meeting reports that the Diocesan Commission that had requested those funds said that it was under misapprehension of the financial state of Saint John's Church. In other words, they said that they believed that the parish had far more funds than it really did – a situation that seems not to have changed much in all the years that have passed!

By April 20, 1868, continuing financial strain led to a resolution which was passed forming a new committee including the Rector who were

"to discreetly ascertain and report to the vestry the most desirable relocation for the church in case a removal is decided upon and also to report on the feasibility and desirability of a sale of the church property at its probable selling value."

One month after the formation of that committee the parish property was sold. But we should note that this was not a quick and easy decision. The idea of selling the parish and moving somewhere else was not new. As seen above, a similar committee was formed eight years earlier in May of 1860 charged with the same tasks.

Baptismal and Communicant records show that the parish was growing in numbers and attendance. So what was the nature of the financial crisis which led to the decision to sell and move? An answer may well be found in the manner in which the parish was established.

The first Rector built the church building using his own funds on property he already owned. The vestry decided at its first meeting on March 2, 1827 to purchase the building and presumably the land on which it stood but did not do so until 1832. From 1827 to 1847 the rector worked for free and the sexton was paid $40 per year, at least in the earlier years. The parish was primarily funded by the sale and rental of pews as were most churches of the day. So expenses were negligible for the first 20 or so years.

However within five years of having to begin paying a rector's salary, financial difficulties began to be reported in vestry minutes, though only obliquely. As reported above, a special committee was appointed in May of 1852 to investigate some mysterious financial matter. A report was received by the vestry in October of that year and at that same meeting the Rector's resignation was accepted. Since the Rector went on to serve other parishes for many years without a hint of scandal, it is doubtful that the financial matter in question was a result of any sort of misappropriation of funds on his part. It is more likely that the matter had to do with a lack of basic funding.

So in May of 1868, only 36 years after purchasing the building and 21 years after the parish began paying the full salary of its Rector, the building and grounds were sold for $90,000.

CHAPTER TWO: RELOCATING THE PARISH

Relocating a parish is never easy. There are always deep bonds of affection that bind people to the buildings in which they were baptized, married, and from which loved ones have been buried. As we have seen from the newspaper account of the reopening of the renovated wooden structure on Johnson Street the old church building was affectionately called the **Church in the Meadows** by those who loved it.[24] We don't know anything about the Meadows in which it was located, but it must have been hard for those who loved that old building to leave it. Some people probably refused to discuss any sort of move while others agreed that the parish needed to relocate in order to reach its potential.

Above all, the leaders of the parish wanted to relocate to a neighborhood with the potential for growth and economic stability, and, since most of them would continue to live near the old church, one that would be accessible by good public transportation. In order to understand the options available to them let's take a brief look at the Brooklyn they knew and how it had developed.

Brooklyn was first settled in the late 1630's and early 1640's by Walloon and Dutch farmers who settled along the shoreline just north of

---

[24] *See End Notes*

the Fort Greene area, and in 1645 the Dutch village was centered where the Brooklyn and Manhattan Bridges now stand. The village developed very slowly and even by 1790, two years after the New York State Legislature incorporated Brooklyn as a town, the population was only 1,603.

The opening of reliable ferry service between Brooklyn and New York caused the first great spurt of development that changed Brooklyn from a quiet town into the third largest city in 19th century America. The first regular ferry service began in 1814 when Robert Fulton's ship Nassau opened a route between New York and Brooklyn. By the mid-1830's and 1840's, fast, safe and reliable steamboats were regularly plying the waters between the two cities making it possible and convenient for a New York City businessman to live in Brooklyn and work in Manhattan.

The extensive residential development of Brooklyn began in the 1830's in the Brooklyn Heights area, which was located near the ferry slips. The rapid growth in the town's population led to the incorporation of Brooklyn as a city in 1834. As the 19th century progressed, the residential area expanded outward in an easterly and southerly direction from the Heights and by mid-century much of the area now lying west of Flatbush Avenue (including the present-day neighborhoods of Brooklyn Heights, Cobble Hill and Boerum Hill) had been substantially built up.

By the early 1850's major residential development was beginning in the area now known as Fort Greene. Fort Greene Park, originally called Washington Park, predates this row house development. The park had been planned in the 1840's (on the site of an old fort) as an open space for the working-class population which then inhabited the area. Most of the houses erected in Fort Greene before the Civil War were fairly modest by comparison with later construction.

These houses included frame dwellings and modest brick and brownstone row houses, many of which are still standing on South Oxford Street, Cumberland Street and Carlton Avenue. The middle-class residents of these houses made the area respectable, and this led to the construction of grander brownstone rows and a number of freestanding mansions (two of which were located on Lafayette Avenue between South Oxford Street and South Portland Avenue, but they have been replaced by apartment houses) for the upper middle class. South Portland Avenue, South Oxford Street and Clermont Avenue became the home of wealthy merchants, lawyers, stockbrokers, and businessmen.

With this influx of a new "monied" population there came a change in the park. By 1867 when Olmsted & Vaux were appointed to lay out the parks of Brooklyn, Washington Park had severely deteriorated. The Olmsted

Design for Prospect Park, circa 1868

& Vaux design for the park was planned to appeal to the leisure time requirements of the middle-class families who were living in the newly built brownstones.[25]

It was quite natural that the leaders of the parish considered this newly wealthy and fashionable community to be a prime candidate for the new structure. Within days of the formal sale of the parish property, an offer of $21,000 for six lots of land on the corner of De Kalb Avenue and Elliott Place was made and accepted.[26] Within a few months an architect, Mr. E.

---

[25] *FORT GREENE HISTORIC DISTRICT*
DESIGNATION REPORT
EDWARD T. KOCH, MAYOR
NYC LANDMARKS PRESERVATION COMMISSION
KENT L. BARWICK, CHAIRMAN
MORRIS KETCHUM, JR., VICE CHAIRMAN

[26] *The church holds a deed now long-defunct for property at the corner of DeKalb Avenue and Elliott Place with a frontage of 359 feet and a depth of 264 feet. According to our records there are two Titles of Deed to this property.*
Therefore it is believed there were actually two parcels of land. One was delivered to a Mr. Thomas J. Taylor and wife on August 5, 1868, by a Mr. James B. Beers, who appears to be at that time the clerk of the vestry, in the amount of $4,000. Another deed dated August 15, 1868, was delivered to a Mr. Louis van Antwerp, Sr. for the purchase price of $19,250. This had to be the money used to buy land on Douglass Street for the new church. In addition, there is evidence of a loan made through the East River Savings

Grand Army Plaza circa 1894

Grand Army Plaza Today

T. Potter, who later designed the current building in Park Slope, was hired to design a new building. But it was never to be built – at least not there.

At the same meeting of the vestry in which the property was sold in May of 1868, an application was received from families residing near another park planned by Olmsted & Vaux asking Saint John's to establish a mission in that part of the city. The vestry enthusiastically accepted this request and resolved that the committee on church property be authorized to select a suitable location for establishing such a mission and that the Rector be requested to commence services there the next Sunday! Within a few weeks a report from the committee on church property that services had begun to be offered in the Chapel of the Home for Destitute Children on Butler Street near the entrance to Prospect Park.

In February of 1869 residents near Prospect Park families who attended those services expressed a strong desire to have Saint John's relocate there, a desire shared by the Bishop of Long Island, who wrote to the vestry that he would prefer that Saint John's Church be built near Prospect Park rather than on the DeKalb property.

In a resolution a few days later, the vestry created yet another committee to select a location in that neighborhood and by February 26 they recommended the purchase of property on the northwest corner of Douglass Street and Seventh Avenue where 10 lots were purchased for the price of $26,000.

Prospect Park, bounded by Prospect Park West, Prospect Park Southwest, Parkside, Ocean, and Flatbush Avenues, consists of 526 acres of rolling meadows, picturesque bluffs, and luxuriant verdure. The park is the chief playground of Brooklyn, with picnic grounds, tennis courts, baseball diamonds, ponds, a zoo, a lagoon, parade grounds, bandstand,

---

Bank for nearly $30,000, presumably borrowed and used for the construction of the chapel and Rectory. No records indicate how or when that debt was repaid.

gravel walks, and broad drives. The city of Brooklyn purchased most of the area in 1859 at a cost of nearly four million dollars from the Litchfield estate, whose mansion serves as borough headquarters of the Parks Department. Delayed by the Civil War, development was begun in 1866 under a commission headed by James S. T. Stranahan, the "Baron Haussmann" of Brooklyn, creator of its park and boulevard system.

Horse-drawn rail cars running between the park and the ferry, brought many rich New Yorkers to the neighborhood transforming it by the 1870's and 1880's into what came to be called the Gold Coast. By 1883, with the opening of the Brooklyn Bridge, Park Slope continued to boom and subsequent brick and brownstone structures pushed the neighborhood's borders farther. The 1890 U.S. Census showed Park Slope to be the richest community in the United States.

Having provided leadership for the purchase of property for the new church, Father Burgess decided to move on with his ministry rather than to stay to oversee the building of the new church. He resigned as Rector in a letter dated October 7, 1869, and shortly thereafter became the Rector of Christ Church in Springfield, Massachusetts, where he served until elected the first Bishop of the new diocese of Quincy, Illinois. The building of the new church was left in the hands of the lay leadership of the parish.

CHAPTER THREE: BUILDING IN THE SLOPE

A letter was written to the Bishop of Long Island requesting that he participate in the laying of the cornerstone for the new building, which was to serve as a place to offer divine services

> *"until such time as the church is erected on the corner of seventh Avenue and Douglass Street."*

The cornerstone of the new chapel was laid June 15, 1869, and it is still to be

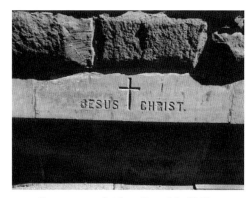

Cornerstone laid on June 15, 1869

seen today on the far left of the steps going up to the Chapel, the original entrance to the church. It reads simply: "Jesus + Christ.

The opening service of the new chapel is reported in the Brooklyn Daily Eagle of January 17, 1870, which says,

"The opening services at the new chapel yesterday morning were attended by about six hundred persons. After the pews had all been filled camp stools were placed in the aisles for those who could not be otherwise accommodated. At half-past ten o'clock Right Rev. A. N. Littlejohn, D. D., Bishop of Long Island, entered the chapel followed by Rev. Robert E. Terry, Rev. A. N. Spafard, Rev. R. R. Johnson, Rev. Mr. Newton and Rev. Mr. Degen. As the clergy advanced up the aisle and took their seats inside the chancel, the choir sang the welcoming hymn commencing "To the glorious King, shall the ransomed people sing."

The usual morning service of the Episcopal Church was then celebrated. The tenth selection of Psalms and Jackson's Te Deum were chanted by the choir. The Ante-Communion service was read by Bishop Littlejohn, the choir chanting the responses ... The sermon was preached by the Right Rev. Bishop Littlejohn ...

On the conclusion of the Bishop's discourse, Rev. Dr. Terry announced that the offertory would be for the benefit of the missions of the city, and while the collection was being taken up the trio "Lift Thine eyes" was sung ....

The Sacrament of the Holy Communion was then administered, after which the Bishop pronounced the benediction and the congregation dispersed.

One can only wonder how on earth they got 600 people inside since only what is now the chapel was completed! The service also marked the beginning of the ministry of the newly called Rector, the Reverend Robert E. Terry.

We are lucky to have this article because it provides us with a wonderful description of the newly constructed buildings that is not found anywhere else and a description of the original plans for a larger structure to be built, which, as it turns out, never was:

"The Chapel is a substantial stone structure of the Gothic style of architecture, and will seat about 400 persons. The interior is very

Stained Glass at Saint John's Church

Top, a collage of our glass. Above left to right, Saint Cecilia, Chapel;
Saint John, Chancel, Geometric Design Series in Nave and one in the
Guild Room recently restored in Loving Memory of the parents of
Father Powers.

The Holy Family Windows in the Nave facing Saint Johns Place

Christ Blessing Children - Tiffany
Guild Room, Saint John's Church

The Lancet Windows over the Chapel Door
Seven windows depicting the Seven Sacraments,
each surmounted by a Saint.

From left to right

Holy Matrimony, Saint Andrew
Holy Ordination, Saint Luke
Holy Penance, Saint Elizabeth
Holy Baptism, Saint John
Holy Communion, Saint James
Holy Unction, Saint Martha
Holy Confirmation, Saint Francis

Once behind the High Altar, these windows featuring Saint
John in the center and two geometric designs on either side
are now partially hidden by organ pipes over the current
location of the choir.

handsomely fitted up, the woodwork being of Oak, and the pretty prevailing colors of the decorations are blue and gold, which contrast very pleasantly with a rich dark brown used on other portions of the building.

The stained-glass windows, which have already done good service at Saint John's church, had been removed to the new edifice, and a Memorial window, bearing the inscription, 'In memory of Reverend Thomas T. Guion, Rector of this church from February 1, 1853, to October 21, 1862', has been placed in the rear of the chancel, where it will remain until the new church is built. The Chapel is also furnished with a fine organ, in which Mister Archibald Arthur, the organist at Saint John's church for a long time past, will preside.

Adjoining the Chapel, on the West side, a Rectory is now in course of erection is also of stone, in the style of architecture will correspond with that of the Chapel. Between Seventh Avenue and the Chapel there are six lots of ground on which it is intended at no distant day to erect a magnificent stone church, and the Chapel will then be used for prayer meetings and other similar purposes. The total cost of the Chapel and Rectory together with the ground has been about $80,000 and it is estimated that the church which it is proposed to erect will cost a similar amount."

Stone, dark wood, with walls of blue and gold – the new Saint John's was certainly Victorian! According to one authority on the Victorian period,

"It was in the 1840's that Gothic Revival, with its Romantic preference for natural dark colors and elaborate ornament, reached New York. Gothic found its ideal building material in the local brown sandstone of Connecticut and New Jersey. Soft brownstone could be cut to produce elaborate facades for brick row houses-and in no time weathered to a rich mahogany, which was considered refined. By the 1860's, brownstone had become the favorite building material of New York City."[27]

White limestone was used for aesthetic contrast for the capstones, a few decorative small columns and door arches. A few broad steps and a large arched entranceway housing heavy oak double doors became a grand

[27] *New York News Magazine, June 27, 1976*

facade with an invitingly lofty entrance. From the street it offered a "come hither" view of the High Altar, which in those days was directly opposite the doors where the choir is currently located.

Alongside and above the main doors of the chapel were placed seven windows symmetrically arranged and filled with geometrically designed stained glass, gradually increasing in length and breadth from the lower ones to the top. This too hints at a spirit of "uplifting" or "reaching for above" which reflects the true spirit of Christ, Our Heavenly King.

At the very top is a modest bellcote made of four white stone columns capped with an A-shaped stone to follow the contour of the roof and the front of the edifice itself.

Originally the Main Entrance, these doors now lead to the Chapel

Such architectural fixtures sometimes contain a bell, but often do not. It is not known whether a bell was ever installed in this one but there had been a small tower and bell in the original wooden building so it may have been brought and installed here though it has long since been removed.

Surviving intact for over 100 years, the bellcote was damaged by a tornado which struck this part of Brooklyn in the fall of 2010. That storm knocked a very large stone cross from over the doorway of Saint

Bellcote: Note the falling keystone caused by the Tornado. It seems to have picked it up and dropped it back down!

Augustine's Roman Catholic Church behind us on Sixth Avenue and hurled

41

a large iron cross from the top of the Presbyterian Church directly in front of us into two parked cars.

Luckily, no one was badly injured, but the angel in our Memorial Garden was cast down and broken while the stone work of the bellcote was weakened so that the keystone arch began to fail. The angel was repaired by Building Chairman Larry Bickford and the Church Insurance Company paid for the restoration

Memorial Garden Angel

of the bellcote and repair of the roof. Since the high winds had blown away a number of shingles which led to leaks inside which damaged the plaster and paint, the insurance company also paid to plaster and repaint the entire nave and transept. The total cost of this was just over $500,000 and the project was completed in May of 2012.

Episcopal Churches often display a cross on the uppermost peak of the building and Saint John's was proud to bear two of them made of marble, one atop the bellcote. It is not known when these crosses fell down or were removed but they have been missing for many years. However, as part of the restoration of the Bellcote in 2012 a lovely stone cross was placed back on the top of the Bellcote and is quite stunning!

Newly repaired bellcote with newly installed cross

Another, made of copper was placed over the entrance to the newly expanded church in 1889. It was blown down by a blizzard one night in the 1960's toppled it to the snowy ground. Copper being fairly valuable then, it soon disappeared and has never been seen since.

A lovely Celtic cross was installed in its place in 2005 in memory of a beloved member of the parish, Mr. Jeffrey Thomas, who had served as a Vestryman, Chorister, and Eucharistic minister and who died unexpectedly of a heart attack at the age of 39. A brass plaque in the Narthex above the entrance is dedicated to him as well.

The inside of the church was rectangular, being approximately eighty feet long by forty feet wide and was rather simple in architecture and design. Probably the most beautiful ecclesiastical appointment was the marble font still in use today, which originally was placed just inside the Chapel doors. It was moved to the Narthex in the 1970's but

Celtic Cross over the Narthex Entrance in memory of Jeff Thomas

has recently been restored to the Chapel so that baptisms, which usually take place during Sunday masses these days, are easily visible to all.

The foundation walls of the old building deserve mention. They encompass the present undercroft or parish hall and are made of granite and other very hard stone, three feet thick. An excavation of it a few years ago reminded one of a mighty, if somewhat small, fortress. This then, was the beginning of the present Saint John's Church in Brooklyn on Saint John's Place, a rather small church extending from the present Lady Chapel to where the choir and organ console are now located.

In contrast, the Rectory seems larger than would be warranted by such a small church building but it was built with the planned larger church in mind. It is rather distinctive in architecture and design, which is obvious to anyone who has seen it either from the outside or from the inside. All exterior window frames, except those on the garden floor, are fashioned of brownstone and limestone cornices with gothic arches. Woodwork for the most part is mahogany and walnut, plainly designed, with gothic archways free of the later Victorian filigree or "gingerbread" fussiness which so characterized decor at the end of the 19th century.

Baptismal Font

Seven fireplaces made of Connecticut white marble were also installed. They too are neat in their

43

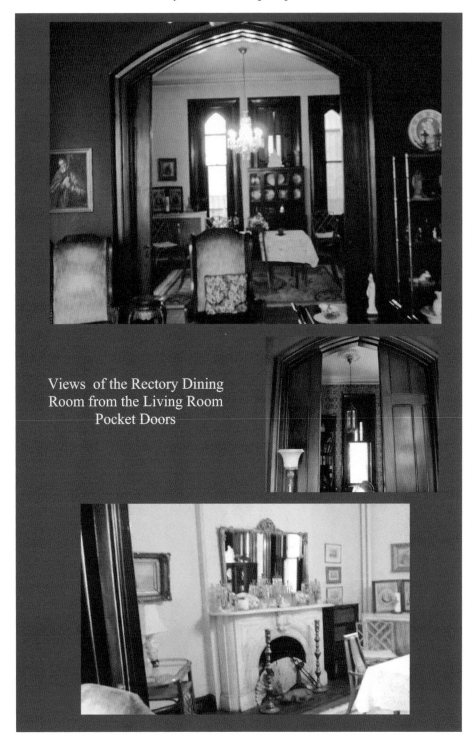

Views of the Rectory Dining
Room from the Living Room
Pocket Doors

The Rectory Staircase and a view of the Living Room

The Rectory Living Room Marble Mantle, one of seven in the house

simplicity rather than commanding attention in a room which they complement, giving it a feeling of spaciousness. Their real purpose was for heating in cold weather, six designed to burn coal and one, in the Dining Room, burned wood. One can only guess what a chore it must have been to tend them day and night, climbing up and down stairs with coal and wood, cinders and ashes so that they were kept clean and tidy, free of soot and smoke.

In addition to the four dwelling floors, a cellar and attic were constructed. The cellar is dark and damp but was no doubt used for laundry and storage of household tools and equipment. The attic is tall enough to stand up in and was used to store boxes and trunks as well as the usual items deemed too good to throw out but not good enough for daily use.

In the beginning, the lower, or garden, floor was occupied by a domestic couple who lived in and, to a large extent, managed the household. The woman would occupy herself with shopping, cooking and light housekeeping, while the man would undertake several roles, among them gardener and liveryman. *(The nearest livery stable was but a block away on the corner of Saint John's Place and Flatbush Avenue.)* The houseman was also called upon for especially heavy chores and for acting as butler from time to time.

Saint John's Church 1869

Above is a photograph of the Chapel and Rectory taken shortly after they were erected. Saint John's Place (then Douglass Street) is seen as a dirt road and all about the immediate buildings are small farm plots. The ornate gaslights and the intricate wrought-iron fencing around the roof have long since disappeared. A view of the churchyard from the Rectory roof in 1870 would have shown a garden, large by current New York standards, comprising all the land on the west side of Seventh Avenue now occupied by the many buildings extending from Saint John's Place to Sterling Place.

The new buildings may have been grand but financial difficulties continued to plague the parish in the new location. The Reverend Terry resigned in January of 1874 but overstayed his welcome in the Rectory and seems to have owed the parish a significant amount of money which they tried to collect and eventually complained in a report to the Bishop that he

"had not delivered to the proper officers of the church the records of the Parish and also that he had failed to pay over money still in his hands and due to the Parish."

The records of the parish seem to have included the Baptismal Register since the one dating to this era is still missing today. Several weeks after his resignation he was apparently still in residence in the Rectory and the Vestry resolved

"The Clerk is directed to communicate these facts to the Reverend Terry and respectfully request that the Vestry be placed in position to give possession of the Rectory on the 1st of March"

so that they could rent it out. He finally left to become Rector of Christ Church in Hudson, New York.

If the end of his tenure at Saint John's was marked with stress, his next posting was a total disaster! Within a year or so he was the center of quite a scandal involving a young lady, 19 years of age, named Miss Ida Farron which led to his resignation there. The Brooklyn

The Reverend R. E. Terry
Seventh Rector

Daily Eagle had quite an article on the episode that states that he

will be remembered by those who knew him here, has a fine commanding presence and is pleasant in his manners and pleasing in his conversation. He is about fifty years of age, and his family consists of a wife and four children, two of the latter being grown up daughters ....

It seems that a few days before his resignation was tendered, a young lady of his congregation, while slightly sick, was being attended by her sister. The sister had occasion to get some articles from a bureau drawer used by the sick girl. In the search a package of letters, carefully done up, attracted her attention. A glance at these showed the sister that they were the production of Rev. Mr. Terry, and they were immediately handed over to her father, who read them with growing rage and indignation. The name of the young lady is Miss Ida Farron, a charming girl in her 19th year.

This trouble, however, will not end here, as the Bishop will likely degrade him from his ministerial functions, Only a few persons have seen the letters, but it is said at the worst they are simply silly and full of love making.

Even though this seems to have been a silly romantic dalliance, it is always sad when someone abuses the trust that is placed in their hands, especially if that person is a trusted pastor. No further information was readily available concerning his fate, but wherever he went he seems to have taken our parish record books with him.

The Reverend Thomas S. Pycott was called to become the eighth Rector in February of 1874 with an annual salary of $1800. At the same vestry meeting which issued the call another motion was passed to rent the Rectory out for $1800 per year leaving the new Rector only a couple of rooms to live in![28]

CHAPTER FOUR: GIVING UP THE DREAM, EXPANDING FOR THE FUTURE

There is an often repeated legend at Saint John's that the parish treasurer absconded with the all parish funds in the late 1870's and lost them in the gold fields of California and that is why the large church which was to be built on Seventh Avenue was never constructed! It is a colorful tale but so far no evidence has been found to corroborate it. However, it is clear that at least by 1885 the dream of building that larger church clearly was not going to happen anytime soon. There were just no funds available.

It is fairly easy to see what happened if you stop and do the math. Saint John's was in debt in 1868 when the old church property was sold for $90,000. How much of that money went to pay off debt we don't know. But within a few days lots were purchased in Fort Greene for $21,000 and a mortgage or loan was taken out for $30,000. These were later sold so probably most of the funds were recovered but it is likely that some costs were incurred. Then a few weeks later 10 lots were purchased for $26,000 on the northwest corner of Douglass Street and Seventh Avenue in Park Slope. When the buildings were opened for services on January 16, 1870 the Brooklyn Daily Eagle newspaper reports that the total cost of the buildings and grounds came to about $80,000. So even if most of the money

---

[28] The legal document states in part that the church agrees to "*Let... the furnished house as per schedule hereto annexed and known as the Rectory of Saint John's Church, Brooklyn, N.Y. on Saint John's Place and next west of Saint John's Chapel, said Household Furniture to be returned to said party of the first part in as good condition as they are received, the natural use and wear thereof excepted, reserving for the Rector the first and second story corner rooms and also the small room in the rear of said house on the first floor.*"

spent in Fort Greene was recovered and used to pay off the mortgage, the $90,000 received from the sale of the old church in 1868 was all spent and gone by 1870. Within four years the vestry and the Rector (Father Terry) were involved in a major dispute over funds and the salary of the next rector could only be paid by renting out the new rectory and leaving him only a couple of rooms for his own use!

The estimated cost of a new and larger church on Seventh Avenue was about $80,000, far beyond the means available. So the lots on Seventh began to be sold and brownstone homes were built ending the dream of a large church on the Avenue. Along with that dream went any possibility of a major expansion which might have included offices, meeting and classroom spaces such are seen in many churches built somewhat later in the neighborhood.

But the chapel, never intended to be the main church, was simply too small. So in February 1885 a committee was formed (composed of three people, James C. Jewett, Eugene L. Herrick and Robert Bagg) to obtain subscriptions to fund the enlargement of Saint John's Church because

> *"we are near the point when the seating capacity of our Church will be inadequate to meet the wants of Episcopalians residing in this neighborhood. As it is, we are continually losing valuable families, for the reason that we have not a sufficient number of low-priced pews to meet the demands."*

The church was crowded and it needed more income. So it was enlarged in order to seat a larger crowd of people at worship who would also bring in much needed revenue.   This is probably why so many churches in the city were built so large – so they could accommodate large crowds on holy days and so that they could increase income throughout the year through the sale and rental of pews.

Saint John's assumed its present cruciform shape when the chancel and the nave were added in 1885. This more than doubled the seating capacity to about 500 people. Inasmuch as the expansion followed so soon after the original construction, the plans and the stone itself matched so perfectly that it is virtually impossible to tell that the whole church as we see it today was not built at the same time and many people comment on first entering the church that it looks so much larger inside than from the street. That is because much of the sanctuary is situated behind the Rectory.

The Rose Window in the new Narthex

A window[29] was placed directly behind the high altar in 1885, which indicates that a cloth curtain (dossal) was fixed behind the altar under that window, or a wooden background (raredos) was used. In any case, the chancel-sanctuary platform was not elevated as it is today. It was no more than a small step above the nave floor, which fact was revealed in this decade

---

[29] *This was the Saint John's Window later moved to tits current location in the Chancel*

Saint John's Church with the new Nave

when, in remodeling the sanctuary a niche was uncovered too close to the present floor to be used for a credence or table for bread, wine and water used in the Holy Eucharist.

The west wall incorporates a large Rose Window of very heavy wooden tracings, containing seven quatrefoil panels of stained glass. The colors that predominate are purple, blue and amber in symmetric patterns with an overall effect of geometric or even floral design. It is not known what studio created the glass work, nor to whom the window was dedicated.

In the nave were placed three prominent arched windows of geometric design on either side at pew level, and above in the roof are four triangular arched windows on each side. Throughout the nave and in the north transept the color tones of the glass were primarily light green and yellow. The hue cast by them at midday was a pale chartreuse color, which was strongly reflected on the surrounding walls.

At the east end of the church, an enclosed porch or vestibule made of stone was to become the new main entrance, housing the original cornerstone of 1827.

The architecture has been described as "early English"; rural Gothic with a Victorian flavor. The architect was Edward Tuckerman Potter, who was engaged even before the property in Park Slope was purchased. He had impeccable ecclesiastical connections: his father was The Right Reverend Abraham Potter, Bishop of Pennsylvania; his uncle, The Right Reverend Horatio Potter, was Bishop of New York; two of his brothers, Philip Nott Potter and Henry Cadman Potter, were priests, and the latter succeeded his uncle as Bishop of New York.

The Church of the Good Shepherd, which he designed on the Colt estate in Hartford, Connecticut, is almost identical in exterior and interior design to Saint John's. Note the design of the slate roof on the picture to the left as it an excellent example of what the roof at Saint John's was like before being replaced with modern shingles in the last century. The crosses above the doorway and crosses on the roof no doubt were also like the ones lost over the years at Saint John's.

*Church of the Good Shepherd
Hartford, CT*

CHAPTER FIVE: GROWING INTO THE NEW LOCATION

The Reverend George F. Breed became the ninth Rector in 1887 and served until 1903. During these sixteen years Park Slope was extensively built up as new homes, shops and churches were added. On our own corner of Seventh Avenue the Methodist Church was built on one side and the Presbyterian on the other between 1885 and 1900.

The Reverend George Breed, Ninth Rector

As the old century ended and the new one began there was a continued excitement and enthusiasm which contributed to the growth and development of the Episcopal Church throughout the nation as well as here in Brooklyn. Sometimes in our modern world we look at statistics of stagnant growth in the past few years and think that it has always been this way. But obviously it has not. 1826, when Saint John's was founded, through 1869 was an amazing period of growth for the Episcopal Church in Brooklyn as 45 new churches were founded and constructed![I]

By 1885 the Episcopal Church throughout the nation was turning its attention to missionary work both here at home in the United States and abroad. Missionary dioceses were founded in the mid-western and western states and territories to serve the growing population of Episcopalians moving into those areas as well as the large number of immigrants from all over Europe who came to work on railroads, farms and factories. Other missionaries were sent out to Africa, South America and Asia. All of this activity was supported by Missionary Chapters in most parishes around the nation including an active one here at Saint John's.

A copy of a periodical entitled ***The Parish*** was found in our records which was printed monthly at Saint John's by the Orphans' Press, operated by boys from a nearby orphanage which was founded and supported by the (Episcopal) Church Charity Foundation. Unfortunately, the only copy that seems to have been saved was the edition from May of 1900. It reports that there were eighteen teachers and 356 children in our parish Sunday School that year in addition to a nursery staff to care for infants during the principal service each Sunday. That would be remarkable for any church of any denomination in today's Brooklyn! It is an example of the sort of enthusiasm which once enlivened the church. One article in that May 1900 edition, reprinted from an English source called **Saint Paul's Church Chronicle**, says:

> *In our American Church there is equal encouragement. The growth of the Church has been remarkable. The seventeen bishops of sixty years ago have increased to ninety; 820 clergy to 4,800. Instead of twenty-one dioceses and jurisdictions there are now eighty. The ration of growth in communicants has far outstripped the increase in population. In the last decade the population increased twenty-four percent, while the increase in communicants was fifty-five percent.*

> *Not until 1835 did the Church seriously undertake missionary work. Then the organization of the Domestic and Foreign Missionary Society was completed with a membership embracing all baptized persons. In the same year the first missionary Bishop, Jackson Kemper, was consecrated and sent to the Northwest. We need not trace the development of missionary life and work since those days, step by step, but we may well note the progress that has been made since 1885, when Dr. Langford, the late secretary of the Domestic and Foreign Missionary Society, was called to and assumed the heavy burdens he bore with such unfailing cheerfulness.*

> *At that time, less than fifteen years ago, the Church was represented in the home and foreign fields by 721 lay and clerical workers. Of these, sixteen were missionary bishops---three abroad, thirteen at home. The number of missionary workers has now risen to 1,630, twenty-three of whom are bishops. In 1885 the gifts for general mission work mounted to $450,175. The appropriations for the current years will require offerings of $630,000.*

As the church was growing it was also beginning to change liturgically. By the middle of the nineteenth century something that came to be called the Oxford Movement, because it began at Oxford University in England, began to influence life in the Church of England. Within a very short time that influence began to be felt here in the United States, especially in New York.

The Oxford Movement was founded upon the belief that the Holy Catholic Church is, or should be, a visible body upon earth bound together by a spiritual unity even though divided administratively. According to this point of view, the Anglican Communion, as a part of that visible body of the ancient Catholic Church, has an intimate and unbroken connection with the early church and its teachings.

The Right Reverend Abram N. Littlejohn, the first Bishop of Long Island

Along with this idea was a desire to revive some of the ancient practices of that ancient church within current liturgical expression. Eventually, colorful Eucharistic vestments, incense, and bells began to return to use in some parishes in the Episcopal Church. Sacramental theology also began to be emphasized and along with that came a desire to make the primary service on Sunday the Holy Eucharist, or as it came to be called in many places, the Mass. This point of view eventually won the day in the United States, but it took some 100 years for it to do!

In the meantime, from the mid-nineteenth to the mid-twentieth century a conflict which came to be called High Church vs. Low Church grew ever louder in many places. The Diocese of Long Island has long been called a High Church diocese by most of the rest of the church. An article by The Right Reverend Abram N. Littlejohn, the first Bishop of Long Island, is entitled *"Catholic Dogma: Its Nature and Obligations"* is an early example of why this was the case since Easter Day is referred to as "*a day of Holy Obligation*, when the Church requires every communicant to receive the Blessed Sacrament." Although most of us today see that as a simple statement of fact, the way it was phrased was perceived by many at the time as being extremely High Church, even **Romish!**

In the midst of this change the church continued to grow in numbers and influence. Architects often say that *form follows function* and so it does in the Church. That is to say, churches are constructed, or renovated, to best serve the sort of worship and other activities offered there. And so it was as the great National Cathedral was planned and began to be built in Washington as a place where great and solemn Masses could be offered. Another, Saint John the Divine, began to take shape in New York City and here in Long Island a beautiful little Gothic gem was constructed in Garden City and named the Cathedral of the Incarnation. All of this would eventually have a big impact on parish life and worship at Saint John's here in Park Slope as would the later impact of a more diverse population. But change comes so slowly in most parishes that it is hardly noticed much of the time and so it was here.

Cathedral of the Incarnation, Garden City, Long Island

Meanwhile, as it grew and developed Saint John's became noted for its music, especially for its boys choir. It was composed of both men and boys and numbered thirty-one persons, including twenty sopranos, three altos, four tenors, and four bassos. The choir belonged to the Choir Guild of the diocese. Elaborate musical services were given at the "mother church," Saint Ann's in Brooklyn Heights, once or twice a year.

The parish also continued to be very involved in outreach and concern for the poor. One aspect of that ministry was focused on the Orphan House mentioned above. In 1900 it provided shelter for thirty children ranging in age from fourteen to eighteen years. They were duty-bound to attend church here each Sunday and sat in the south transept. Rather naturally, these benches were known as orphans' pews.

~~Saint Giles Home~~ *for Crippled Children*

Saint John's choir also entertained twice a year on Sunday afternoons at Saint Giles Home for Crippled Children[30] and at Saint John's Home for the Aged. The cost of burial was often too high for people in need so the parish also provided free burial plots for the poor in a portion of The Evergreen Cemetery which was consecrated and set aside as the Saint John's Burial Ground.[31]

[30] *The House of St. Giles the Cripple was founded in 1891 by Sister Sarah, an Episcopalian nun. http://www.stgilesfoundation.org/story.php*
http://thehistorybox.com/ny_city/nycity_homeless_st_giles'_home_1893_article00754. htm ; Brooklyn Daily Eagle September 3, 1893

CHAPTER SIX: MAKING DO

The first part of the twentieth century at Saint John's might be described as a time of "Making Do" or perhaps a time of "Doing More with Less." During this time, several new organizations were formed in the parish, but they had little room to meet or to conduct their activities. The

Saint John's Sunday School 1914

worship space had been expanded shortly before the 19th century came to a close but as the 20th century dawned it became apparent that more space was needed for all the other activities of the parish. According to our records, shortly after the turn of the century the Sunday School numbered

---

[31] *When City Park, near the Brooklyn Navy Yard was constructed, bodies from a cemetery existing at that site were removed to The Evergreens Cemetery. To compensate the churches which had some claim to the ground where those bodies were buried, plots in the new cemetery were assigned to each denomination. The Honorable Edwin M. Grant was clerk of the vestry and also by chance city comptroller at that time and he secured a ruling that gave the Episcopal space in The Evergreens Cemetery equally to Saint John's and Saint Ann's as the two original Episcopal churches in Brooklyn. Many plots were made available free to those in need. Up to four people could be buried in each plot and many were. There are no single plots left though there may be a few spaces available in shared graves.*

349 children with fifteen teachers but there were no classrooms and only a low ceilinged and rather dingy basement room, so one has to wonder where these classes were taught!

There were the thirty-one choir members but no Music Office or rehearsal space. The Altar Guild, Mission Guild, and many other organizations of the parish had to meet wherever they could find an unoccupied corner. The Guild Room and what is now the outer Sacristy were the only two rooms available for all of this activity other than the church itself and the unfinished basement where a team of men and boys had to work pumping the noisy bellows during services so that the organ had enough air to play! But since the adjacent lots had been sold there was no space to build outward even if money had been available.

What money was available beyond the ordinary expenses of the parish had to be spent to reduce the debt and to keep the buildings and grounds in good condition. Without an occasional large donation few needed repairs could have been done. One great expense faced by the vestry was replacement of the public sidewalk. The old-fashioned, pot-holed tar sidewalk had to be replaced at a cost of $1,500 – a great deal of money in those days. Luckily, an anonymous donor not only came to the rescue, but supplied enough additional funds to install a beautiful new ceiling in the church.

From 1903 to 1911 the Reverend Frank D. Page served as the ninth Rector. He and Mrs. Page were both from the South, and entertained with truly Virginian hospitality. They were also the first to raise children in the rectory. He and his family brought to the parish a great sense of hope that things would get better. The spirit of the nation itself, at this time, was one of courage and national advancement. It was characterized by the rough-riding President Theodore Roosevelt, who is remembered as the man with the "big stick."

As a result of the Spanish American War, the United States came to control vast new colonial possessions and to exert power and influence throughout the Western Hemisphere and as far away as Asia. New inventions including the automobile and even the airplane began to transform the way people lived. Manufacturing plants began to spring up seemingly everywhere to make new products to sell not only here but also in the new colonies and around the world. A new sense of confidence pervaded in the nation and that seems to also be the case here at Saint John's.

It was during this time that Park Slope became home to an ever growing population of the very wealthy and the upper middle class. Elegance and propriety became the fashion of the Slope and it was not found to be lacking in the rectory. A lady communicant, Mrs. Marguerite Sadtler, who had been raised in this neighborhood from early childhood, remembers its gracious hospitality. She recalls visiting the Pages for high tea on Sunday afternoon as a little girl. Her place was standing behind her mother's chair in a lovely rectory parlor softly aglow with candlelight from a chandelier and wall sconces, attended by maids attired in the traditional black uniform with white, starched, lace-decorated aprons and caps. This setting would be romantic, if a bit "stiff," in any age, and one has to wonder where the funds came from for such elegant living. Perhaps the Page family were wealthy in their own rite since the salary being paid to him was not so very large. At any rate, not long after this time, Doctor Page's health began to suffer, and he returned to his native Virginia, which he loved so well.

The Reverend Thomas Bond Holland became the eleventh rector of Saint John's in 1911. The predominant worry for the new rector and his vestry was meeting the $30,000 debt still owing on the present buildings. But the continued need for more education and activity space caused them to spend a great deal of time fund raising, not only to pay the debt but to expand a bit. As we have seen, the adjacent lots having been sold, there was no place to go but down!

The parish leadership also made use of money which had accrued in something called the Cemetery Fund to finance the repairs of the rather dark and dingy basement to create a larger, though still low ceilinged, multipurpose room and small kitchen. These had to serve as the main areas for activities and education until the more extensive renovations more than a half century later.

In 1925, fourteen years after his arrival at Saint John's, Father Holland married a lady who was not only from Brooklyn, but also a member of the parish. It must have been a grand and ceremonial wedding that took place in the church on June 23, 1925, between T. Bond Holland, priest and rector, and Dorothy Hill Pierce. But it must have become apparent as that grand event took place that the church was greatly in need of new paint.

Funds were raised to paint and plaster in time for the centennial anniversary of Saint John's in 1926. An historian named Mr. Fred Clarke was asked to prepare a sermon for the 100th anniversary, which he did with great eloquence. His reflections have also provided some of the information upon which this history is based.

Though finances were still tight, economically speaking, these were boon years for the parish and many years would pass before funds would be available to do any further repairs, let alone decoration. Fortunately, the Rector and vestry managed to pay off most of the outstanding parish debt before the worst of the Great Depression hit the parish and nation in 1929 and the years that followed. Father Holland resigned in 1930 and died a few months later here in Brooklyn. Beautiful brass flower vases for the High Altar were given in his honor and are inscribed simply: T. Bond Holland, M.D., 1911-1930. One of these is on display in a lovely oak and glass display case in the Guild Room, the other having been lost by one of our florists.

Traditionally, Episcopal Churches are not consecrated until their mortgages have been paid off. Thanks to the diligence of Father Holland and the parish leadership the mortgage was finally paid off in 1931 just in time for the arrival of the new rector, The Reverend Gordon D. Pierce. On the Feast of Saint John in December of that same year the Right Reverend Ernest M. Stires, Bishop of Long Island, made an official parish visitation to the parish to consecrate the building at a Solemn Mass of Dedication and Consecration.

It was a beautiful occasion and the official burning of the mortgage was joyously celebrated by all. But 1931 brought lean and tough times to the parish and the nation. Many people and many parishes were burdened with terrible financial losses and the nation was stricken with growing unemployment.

During those years Father Pierce's salary was meager and not always paid. Sometimes it was paid in foodstuffs when they were available. But it seems that God sent the right sort of pastor for those hard economic times. He was known to many as a kind and helpful counselor and always seemed to radiate a sprightly and radiant countenance to all the people he served in the parish and the wider neighborhood.

The future for this church was precarious as the Depression squeezed more and more tightly. Offices and classrooms were still needed, but this was not a time to consider building expansion. It was more a time for meeting the needs of the hungry and needy. There was no social safety net for those who lost jobs and homes. Social Security and Unemployment Insurance had not been invented yet. So the only help available to most people came from churches and other religious institutions.

A chapter of the Diocesan Women's Auxiliary was formed here at Saint John's to raise funds to feed the hungry and provide for the needs of the poor. In addition to helping those in physical need, the church also had to provide for the spiritual needs of people young and old. Father Pierce offered services of worship and a Mister William S. Limond, Jr., the superintendent of the Sunday School, became instrumental in training young minds in the church's catechism, meeting in a room named in his honor, the

William Limond Guild Room. Since there is no plaque reminding people of that name it has all but been forgotten and the room is now usually simply called The Guild Room.

World War II and New Challenges

The Second World War, with all its tragedy, also brought with it a prosperity which lifted the nation out of the doldrums of that terrible depression. No one who lived through those war years will forget the blackouts and brownouts or the air-raid wardens who took their work so seriously. These were often highly respected retired men selected from the citizenry of communities throughout the land. The Civil Defense Department used the boiler room at Saint John's as a storage place for stretchers, blankets, canes and crutches, battery-powered lights, and hard hats. The undercroft itself was labeled an air-raid shelter and the equipment remained in place there until the early 1960's.

It is interesting to note that the parish records do not include any burials during the period of the war years of people who died as a result of injuries suffered in combat. However, unlike today, in that war bodies of those killed in action were most often buried in cemeteries near the fields of battle. A Memorial Plaque containing the names of many who served in the war from Saint John's was uncovered in the Undercroft when Father Powers first became Rector in 1987. It was put aside for cleaning so that it could be hung in the Guild Room but seems to have disappeared in the clean out of the boiler room some years later when asbestos was professionally removed from the facility.

Though we don't have records of the names of those who served, there is no doubt that the war impacted the whole life of this parish as it did communities throughout the nation. Sons, brothers, husbands and no doubt women as well went off to serve the nation's defense. Others worked long and hard hours in the many war industries here in Brooklyn and also in the nearby strategically important Brooklyn Navy Yard. Times continued to be hard and people here rose to meet the challenges as they did throughout the nation.

Very little improvement was made to the church property during the Depression or in the war years since there were few funds available and, at least during the war, no building materials available. Until fairly recent years, Saint John's had no endowment money of any kind and had to live solely on the donations of its people. And during the Depression and war years those donations were very small. The fabric of the church and rectory deteriorated woefully in those years of neglected maintenance. Both buildings were dark and dingy, in need of plaster, paint, plumbing repairs and electrical updating. Windows were so loose in both buildings that the wind could literally be felt blowing fiercely through the structures! But what could not be cured, as they say, had to be endured.

Father Pierce served and suffered through those years and finally left Saint John's to become Rector of a small parish in Vermont in 1950. He had been greatly loved by members of the parish and people of all faiths within the community and would be greatly missed. Perhaps the vestry missed him most of all since they faced a serious problem in seeking a replacement. There was literally no money for repairs to the highly neglected buildings and only with the greatest effort could a tiny salary of $4,000 per year could be offered. I think it can be stated fairly clearly that priests were not standing in line to come to work here!

Three faithful lay members of the parish deserve honorable mention in this book for the work they did in those very hard days. Doctor Victor Grover, who lived just a few doors from the church, Mr. William Greve, and the aforementioned Mister William S. Limond held this parish together and managed to attract the Reverend Howard G. Clark who became Rector in 1950. They continued to work with him to organize the finances of the parish and conduct needed repairs bit by bit even as the vital tasks of ministry, teaching and outreach continued to be offered to the neighborhood.

On top of all the other very basic financial needs, the old church boiler was beyond repair, and money had to be found at once to replace it. So Mr. Greves, using the bible as his inspiration, developed a rather clever device to raise funds. Every adult parishioner was given a brand-new one dollar bill and was asked to put into practice the Bible parable of the talents. Each person was told to multiply the dollar by any means and to return the proceeds on a given date. At that gathering each one was to produce his profits and explain how they were earned. Mr. Greve volunteered to match the proceeds dollar for dollar. It was an enjoyable evening and a profitable one too.

The exterior of the church and rectory were in a very sad state of disrepair and needed desperately to be re-pointed with mortar. Bricks on the east wall, where the Rose Window is located, were so loose they could be removed by hand and many were by vandals before they could be repaired. Inside, the old cloth-covered wiring was a serious threat to life and property and had to be replaced for a total cost of $16,000, a very great deal of money in those days. However, the cost did include the ornate iron lanterns hanging inside and those over the doors on the outside. To top it all off, literally, the old slate roof had to be replaced. Unfortunately the slate was removed at a fairly high cost and replaced by less expensive but also less long-lasting modern shingles. Since that time the shingles have been replaced every twenty years or so. If the cost of this constant replacement were added together it might well have cost less in the long-term to have repaired the slate! But as well intentioned as they are most of the time, vestries and rectors are often more concerned with current cost than long time savings. But then again, maybe we just have to be in order to make ends meet!

Christ the King

In addition to these more mundane, but necessary repairs, Father Clark and the parish leadership installed a small chapel altar in the north transept. A cabinet-maker in the parish made the altar which is still in use today. Originally it had a dossal curtain behind it made of deep red velvet with gold brocade trim which was a gift from Saint Paul's Chapel of Trinity Church, Wall Street. It had originally been used there behind the Blessed Sacrament Altar. A polychrome wooden crucifix of Christ the King was given by the Women's Auxiliary of Saint John's in 1952 to hang as an altarpiece in front of this beautiful curtain. But, even though the Oxford movement had influenced the church as a whole a great deal in its one hundred year-history, there were still many battles to be fought between "High" and "Low" Churchmen. One small but loud skirmish was fought right here literally over the Body of Christ! The Rector received such a barrage of discontent about *"romish nature"* of the corpus or body hanging on the cross, clothed in Eucharistic Vestments, that it was removed from the cross and has not been seen since.

This whole controversy probably seems very strange to those Episcopalians reading this book today that this is perhaps a good place to digress for a moment from the particular history of this church and consider the implications of the history of the wider church upon this more particular parish history. In 1952 most Episcopalians were white, upper middle class, and conservative. Morning Prayer (a service that most of our young people today have rarely even seen) was the major service of worship most Sundays in most of our parishes. Eucharistic vestments were seldom used in most parishes and incense was a rare and exotic substance! All of this began to change in the decade of the 1960's as the Church became involved in the civil rights movement. Many conservatives left the church and many liberal Roman Catholics and others joined the church. This editor was one of them, having converted to the Episcopal Church in 1968 while in college.

Converts brought their own history and spirituality with them that began to influence the churches in which they worshipped. During this same era, the Roman Catholic's Vatican II began to have a great influence not only on that church but on all other liturgical churches as well, each of which began to experiment with more liberal versions of liturgical expression. As the Church began to embrace the anti-war movement of the late 1960's and early 1970's more conservatives left the Episcopal Church and more liberals from other denominations, especially the Roman Catholic Church, came to us, causing the church to change even more as they did. Statistics of those days indicated that the Episcopal Church did not grow in numbers. But as is often the case, statistics failed to show what was really happening behind the scenes.

In fact though the statistics might seem to indicate that the decades of the 1960's and 1970's were a time of numerical stagnation in the Episcopal Church, the very opposite was true. Even as it lost many conservative members it gained an equal number of more liberal members who brought new challenges and new visions to an aging structure! As the Church became much more racially and economically diverse so it also became more socially liberal and at the same time more liturgically traditional in worship! By 1976 the Episcopal Church had experimented with a variety of liturgies which had produced the most radical change ever seen in its new *Book of Common Prayer.* After the adoption of the new book in 1976, liturgical change accelerated even more rapidly.

For the first time the *Book of Common Prayer* declared that the major service on Sunday in all parishes would be the Holy Eucharist. As parishes celebrated this Sacrament week after week most began to adopt Eucharistic vestments and some of the other trappings once known only in so-called "High Churches". Within a few years the once familiar terms "High" and "Low" were almost never used since the liturgical traditions that they described merged together to form something new and more vibrant.

All of these changes on a national level had their impact upon this parish of Saint John's in Park Slope. Having moved into a prominent neighborhood of conservative upper middle class people, for awhile Saint John's forgot its roots in that small wooden church built by a radical liberal priest who welcomed everyone to its altars. In the early 1950's when the greatest subject of discussion in the parish was whether or not to have a crucifix of any sort in the church, immigrants from the West Indies were beginning to arrive in ever-increasing numbers. But, to our shame, they were not always welcomed by everyone in the parish. Of course they could come to worship and they did so in slowly increasing numbers. But they were often subtly reminded that they should remain in their "place".

One dear lady named Ismay Watson told this editor that she came to Saint John's in those days and wanted to join the Altar Guild. After a bit of discussion the good ladies of the Guild agreed to hire her to be the Guild "Laundress". That way she could serve but they didn't have to officially make her a member of the Guild, and perhaps in time she would just go away. However they underestimated Mrs. Watson and they misread the future of the church. Mrs. Watson stayed and in time became a beloved member of the Guild and of the parish even as most of those white ladies moved away or died and were replaced by one of the most diverse congregations in the Diocese of Long Island.

Today, Saint John's is once more the racially diverse parish it was initially built to be. At the same time as that change in demographics was taking place the way we worship here also began to change, slowly at first. The controversy over the crucifix was only one of the battles in the struggle that change was begetting.

The gold-leafed cross, minus the corpus, was moved to the vesting sacristy where it now hangs over the cabinet which houses the stoles and other Eucharistic Vestments, which some used to think of as "***too romish***"! And they are used in every service here at Saint John's Church!

In the 1960's the dossal curtain and bare cross were removed so that the existing window behind them could be closed up to provide a niche for a lovely statue of Our Lady donated in the memory of two mothers in the parish, Anna Kuhel and Deloris Derrick. Now this side chapel has come to be called the "Lady Chapel". It was only 10 years or so since the "skirmish of the cross" was fought but by then the old Low Church disapproval of statues had dissipated and the statue of Our Lady was welcomed and has become a beloved fixture in the church.

The gold-leafed cross, minus the corpus

A wooden polychrome tabernacle to house the Blessed Sacrament, was also given as a memorial. It is embellished inside with a gold silk brocade veil and was in use for a few years until the current tabernacle was constructed in the Chancel near the main altar in the 1970's. It is now stored in the sacristy and is used on Maundy Thursday for the Altar of Repose, and on that occasion, is graced with a white silken veil and a golden crown. A very heavy wrought iron communion rail and credence table completed the furnishings of the Chapel.

Wooden Tabernacle for the Chapel

Originally dedicated to the Blessed Sacrament, the chapel was consecrated by the Right Reverend James P. De Wolfe, Bishop of Long Island. The leaflet for that service, held on 16 September 1951, expressed the hope that the seven windows above the chapel door (which had been brought from the original wooden Saint John's building) would someday, God willing, be filled with stained glass to represent each of the Seven Sacraments. This prayer and dream came true some fourteen years later when windows depicting seven saints and the seven sacraments were installed in 1965. The chapel was open to the public

The Lady Chapel Altar set for Maundy Thursday

all day long for meditation and rest. Would that it could be today!

The window which had been closed up behind the statue of the Blessed Virgin was perhaps one of the oldest stained glass windows in the church. It matches those which are in the wall separating church from the Guild Room today. These windows probably were brought here from the old wooden structure in Brooklyn Heights. Funds were raised in 2005 to have these windows taken out, repaired and then reinstalled by a local Park Slope stained glass artist so that they glow with great beauty.

A few years later the window long closed up was beginning to fall apart. Father Powers and several other donors raised funds to have it removed and repaired. It was then installed in the Guild Room in memory of Father Powers'

The Agnes and Clarence Powers
Memorial Window
in the Guild Room

parents, Agnes and Clarence. It replaced a plain glass window in that room and provides a colorful glow to enhance the beauty of the room. It was blessed by Bishop Provenzano on his first visit to Saint John's Church in 2010.

In addition to rebuilding and renovating the parish buildings, new life was being pumped into the old structure as new institutions were created to serve the church and the world including an active chapter of the Brotherhood of St. Andrew for men and boys and a Girls Friendly Society for women and girls. In many ways their activities resembled those of the Boy and Girl Scouts with the added practice of prayer and devotion. A YPF or Young People's Fellowship was also founded for older teenagers which met weekly on Fridays or Sundays. At one point in the 1960's the group attracted so many young people from the neighborhood that it had to be limited to thirty-five active members. There were more than one hundred others who wanted to join. Perhaps its popularity had something to do with the fact that there was a juke-box dance held every Friday night in the Undercroft, open to all the youngsters of the community!

All this was accomplished with God's help and the generosity of the people of the congregation and the community. These were five very busy years of ministry and building. The rectory was also a rather busy place, for Father Clark and his wife had five young daughters. Upon meeting Father Buck for the first time Mrs. Clark made a comment which bears repeating, she said, *"We love this rectory because it always sings."* Father Clark left Saint John's to become Dean of the Cathedral in Harrisburg, Pennsylvania, in 1955. He later joined the staff of the Philadelphia Divinity School and he eventually was made executive director of the Episcopal Church Building Fund. He died at an early age in the springtime of 1975.

Father James Gardner
Fourteenth Rector

By the time that Father Gardner came here to be Rector in 1955 the neighborhood had changed a great deal. The lovely old brownstones of our neighborhood were beginning to show signs of age and many were sold as the families that owned them began to move to the suburbs. After the war many whole communities were built at one time around the central cores of cities providing those with means and a car the opportunity of owning a house with a garden and a garage within easy commuting distance of work. The homes in older neighborhoods such as Park Slope were often converted into smaller apartments or rooming houses. This meant that the population of the neighborhood grew rapidly but the people moving into the rooming houses and small apartments usually had far less income than those who had moved out.

So even as the numbers of children and youth activities grew due to the larger number of children in the community, the funds to support these ministries and to keep the church buildings in good repair were smaller than before. Although a great deal had been done to repair the ravages to the structures that resulted from massive neglect during the years of the Depression and war, the church and rectory buildings were still in sore need of plaster, paint and general sprucing up. An Interior Decoration Fund was established which eventually reached the sum of $21,000, part of which was spent on needed repairs to the Rectory while most went to redecorate the Church worship space.

On 14 April 1956 Father Gardner was married in Engelwood, New Jersey, to a Miss Janet Elizabeth Washburn. He left Saint John's in 1958 to become rector of Saint Barnabus in Ardsley, New York, and in May of that same year, The Reverend Clifford Allen Buck was called to become the fifteenth Rector of the parish, although he was not formally instituted as such until February 1959, when Bishop De Wolfe visited Saint John's for that specific purpose. It occurred on a weekday evening, which made possible the presence of many clergymen from the neighborhood and the Episcopal Churches of Brooklyn. Three former Rectors, Fathers Pierce, Clark, and Gardner, came to participate; the first and only time in our history that a Rector and three former Rectors have celebrated the mass together!

Father Clifford Buck
Fifteenth Rector

The work of redecoration and renovation of the old structures continued as Father Buck took up his duties. After having offered services for the first few weeks of his ministry in the undercroft, he was delighted to finally move back upstairs into a beautifully redecorated worship space. The nave was newly plastered and painted a very pale green.

The chancel ceiling arches, where three glorious angels are painted in oil, were embellished with twenty-two carat gold leaf by two artisans from Italy. In keeping with the style of the day and to the distress of many members of the parish today, the high altar itself and its oak raredos were bleached to a blond honey color popular at that time. The wooden tabernacle door was replaced with a golden door depicting the Lamb of God holding the Resurrection Banner, seated on the Book of Life with its seven seals, so beautifully described in the Apocalypse or the Book of Revelation by Saint John the Divine, our own patron. In each corner of the door there is a sparkling amethyst stone, again mentioned by Saint John. Comfortable new red damask cushions were placed in every pew. Unfortunately, in subsequent years these have become hard and quite uncomfortable. An effort was begun a few years ago to have them cleaned and stuffed with new foam but was soon abandoned as it turned out to be a dirty job and no one wanted to do it! Perhaps someday funds will be found to replace them with something new and more comfortable.

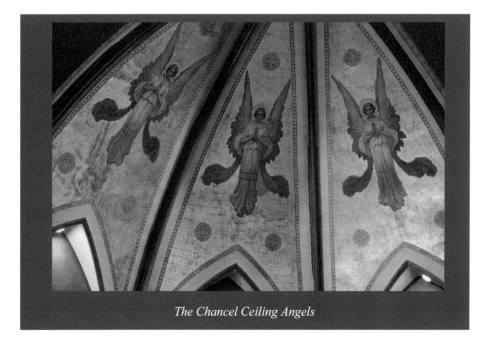

The Chancel Ceiling Angels

In 1960, Dr. Victor Grover, who had served the church so faithfully as a lay leader for many years, secured a gift of $20,000 from an anonymous donor to replace the old 1893 Jardine tracker pipe organ with something better. This served as the basis for an Organ Fund which grew so that in 1962 a new organ was built and installed by the Hillgreen-Lane Organ Builders of Ohio. It was a two-manual, fourteen-rank pipe organ with two sections exposed in the sanctuary arches, a solid oak console with draw-knobs, a set of tubular chimes. The organist at the time was Mr. Keith Verhey who also worked in other areas of the entertainment industry, as is still the case with many talented people in church choirs in New York today. He staged and directed night club shows in Manhattan but still had a great love for the classical music he had studied at Juilliard. So he promised to play a classical concert at St. John's if money could be found to purchase and install a new organ.

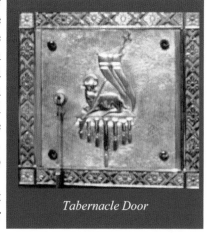

Tabernacle Door

The installation of the instrument covered a span of nine months, far longer than expected, but it was finally dedicated by Archdeacon Saunders at a Sunday afternoon recital played by Keith on 1 April 1962. A small brass plaque on the console bears the inscription: *"In grateful memory, William M. Blake, R.I.P., 1963,"* the name of the original anonymous donor.

By the mid 1960's major liturgical changes that had begun at Vatican II in Rome began to reshape liturgy and the spaces in which liturgical worship was offered in churches around the world. Altars were moved out so that priests and people faced one another as they offered worship together. In 1966 the organ console and choir pews were moved from the chancel here at Saint John's to the north transept. With the advent of plainer and freer sanctuaries and free-standing altars, it was believed that worship would be enhanced with a spacious sanctuary, one that would afford the worshipers a feeling of closeness to the altar, not separated from it by choir and acolyte pews. The music and the choir itself would be an auxiliary or adjunct to public worship and not a focal point of every service.

The director of music at the time was Mr. Steve Empson, whose pleasure with the new arrangement inspired him to seek any means possible to enlarge the size, tone, and scope of the fairly new organ. To that end he applied his talents and most generous and painstaking labor. Ambitious specifications were drawn up, greater than he or the Rector thought would materialize. Little by little, with vastly more desire and hope than money, the expansion was inaugurated, often unseen by the congregation, and requiring labor that lasted well into the morning hours. Some money came from the Altar Guild's Book of Remembrance, and some from quiet individual donations. The two largest factors contemplated were the erection of a third division or housing which would utilize a large section of the sacristy above head level and become the "swell" or "enclosed" organ. The chancel organ could then be divided into two divisions, one called the "great organ" and the other the "positif." This in turn necessitated the redoing of the console, from which the music is played. Three divisions in an organ require three keyboards or manuals.

The church was given a $10,000 legacy to be used at the rector's discretion. Caught up with the notion of having one of Brooklyn's finest contemporary organs, after discussion with the vestry Father Buck then assigned the money to this musical renovation project. No company name can be attached to the present organ, for it represents a compilation of many sources, and though it is unique for that reason alone, it is nonetheless one of great beauty. A series of Sunday afternoon recitals with guest organists from such divergent places as Rochester, New York, and Liverpool,

England, was presented almost bimonthly for a span of two years to celebrate its completion.

Moving the choir and organ was but the first step in the liturgical revision of the worship area at Saint John's to conform better to the liturgical norms of the church throughout the nation and world. Within a short time our main altar was moved out from the wall. Some small steps were removed to provide a spacious platform, which was covered with carpeting and the altar was moved forward and partially rebuilt so that it is now crowned with a beautiful polished marble slab.

Eventually the painting of the seated Christ in Majesty on the wall over the altar was painted over and replaced with a nine-foot linden wood crucifix of the Risen Christ, carved in Oberammergau, Germany, in 1970. The figure is slightly highlighted in pastel colors to dramatize the role with which He is most often depicted. All the heavy wood paneling behind the altar was removed to afford the loftiness and simplicity which we see today. The arches leading into the chancel which contain the organ pipes are covered with a rich blue damask. The altar rails were also reconfigured so that they no longer obstruct the view or entrance to the altar but rather frame the worship area on each side. This lends a feeling of openness to the whole chancel space and makes in more unified with the worshipping congregation.

A few months later, in September of 1971, the Right Reverend C. Alfred Voegeli, exiled Bishop of Haiti, and a dear friend of Saint John's, dedicated a shrine of the Blessed Mother housed in the east wall of the church directly beneath our Rose Window.

The Risen Christ

Baptism Font in its original position near what is now the Chapel Door.

It is a warm and lovely representation of Our Lady, standing serenely with the Christ Child in her arms. Like the crucifix above the altar, it was sculptured in wood by craftsmen from Germany, with a light oak triptych-like background. It was given as a memorial to Anna L. Kuhel by her son, Ron.[32]

Votive candle racks and a "pre-dieu" or prayer desk were placed in front of this shrine making it a place of devotion and not just another artifact to decorate a church building. There prayers were made in private for reasons which are in most cases known only to the Lord, and they are made in union with her who, being the Mother of the Son of Man, is cherished as the spiritual mother of all mankind. People and piety at Saint John's had changed a great deal since the "skirmish of the cross" mentioned above! This shrine later was moved to form the Lady Altar as discussed above.

While all of this was taking place or being planned upstairs, renovation of the undercroft was also planned to take place in stages. First, the main room was painted and decorated with murals. Then the stage (which has since been removed) was supplied with theatrical curtains. Handsome easy chairs and folding chairs and tables were procured for the hall itself.

Nearly every undertaking has a pitfall or two, and the second stage of the undercroft renovations was no exception. In creating the new stairway and door to be found near today's restrooms, a very large boulder was found in excavating and breaking through the original thirty-six-inch foundation wall. After three days of attempting to break it up with air hammers, the workmen gave up and instead dug a hole great enough to bury it below the needed space. In all it required six working days of three men! Only then could the door and the restrooms be installed!

Finally the auditorium was divided into three sections with beautiful but heavy Philippine mahogany accordion folding doors. The entire undercroft was provided with recessed lighting and tile flooring and the

---

[32] *Every year until his death, in about 1999, her son Ron sent money from his home in San Francisco to purchase flowers for this shrine on Mother's Day.*

walls were covered with pecan wood paneling. The total cost was nearly $40,000 and it was a very handsome space.[33]

Even as all this work was going on in the Church and Undercroft, the Rectory continued to deteriorate until parts of it had become very dangerous. It was not out of neglect, of course, but for lack of any money to maintain it through those memorable lean years of the Depression. By 1963 the Rectory kitchen floor was so dangerously weak that the contractor advised that the clothes washer not be used for fear of its dropping to the cellar! The metal ceiling had rusted and given way in places, and immediate attention was absolutely necessary. A bequest of $10,000 from William Greve was earmarked for that purpose. After six months of extensive remodeling, Saint John's Rectory had a new and completely modern kitchen complete with panel walls and appliances. Ten years later, in 1972, a new heating boiler was installed in the Rectory and all the bathrooms were modernized. Like so many other repairs to our historic buildings over the years, this was accomplished by means of an unexpected and very generous legacy, about which there is a brief but interesting story.

The first funeral conducted by Father Buck, a few days after he arrived in 1958, was that of a man in the parish who was survived solely by his elderly wife. Her circumstances thereafter seemed so meager, both socially and financial, that he encouraged her to become actively involved in parish activities, especially in the Women's Auxiliary, and she was invited to call at the rectory any day at noontime to share a bite to eat and for a bit of socializing. After a year or two she disappeared, and the church knew nothing of her circumstances or her whereabouts. Fourteen years later a lawyer contacted the Rector, asking for his services in the burial of Mrs. Agnes Brown. It was then revealed that her monetary assets had been bequeathed to Saint John's. This $27,000 inheritance was used in good part in the renovation of the Rectory, which had been offered to her so long before as a place of respite. It was put to good use!

So the church, the undercroft and the Rectory all received a great deal of attention and repairs in the mid to late 1900's. But the need for adequate meeting spaces and classrooms continued to be unmet. To address this need in a small way the large room which adjoined the main floor of the church, known for many years as the memorial room (no one seems to know just when this flat roofed addition to the church was built nor to whom it was designed to be in memory of!) was divided in 1974, with the larger

---

[33] *Eventually these doors proved too heavy and they pulled from their tracks after a few years. They have now been replaced with portable dividers that roll and fold out as needed.*

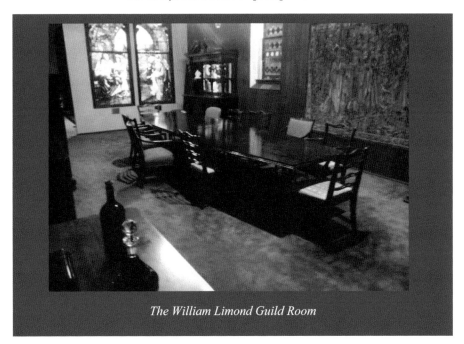

The William Limond Guild Room

section being paneled in wood, carpeted, and graced by two magnificent brass and crystal chandeliers imported from Spain. One of these fell a few years later and was placed in storage in the boiler room until it could be repaired. It is still there! The other, however, was moved to the center of the room and provides lovely and adequate lighting. A family in the parish presented a splendid heavy oak break-front and a huge mirror-backed china cabinet to the parish which are now beautifully placed in this room. The newly decorated and furnished room was blessed during the Solemn Mass of Palm Sunday in 1975 and as mentioned earlier, named the William S. Limond, Jr. Guild Room.

In 1989 a beautiful Tiffany Stained Glass window was donated to the Church by Mrs. Jill Reintjes. Funds were donated to restore this window and place it into a light box in the inner wall of the Guild Room by Mrs. Ivy Latchman. [34] This beautiful room still serves the parish as a much needed

---

[34] *Although I had only been Rector a few months the donation and installation of this window serves as a constant reminder to me of the wonderful diversity of this parish. Ms. Reintjes was a white woman who had purchased this heavily damaged window at auction after the Church of the Messiah burned. It was in boxed up in pieces and the cost of restoring it was about $15,000. We accepted the window with gratitude but told Ms. Reintjes that we had no money to restore and install it. It was stored in the boiler room until a few weeks later when a black lady came into my office and said she would like to purchase a Stained Glass window in memory of some family members but she only had*

meeting area and is now an attractive walk through to the staircase connecting the church floor to the undercroft. As stated above, a second stained glass window was installed in memory of Father Powers' parents.

As can be seen, a great deal of energy was expended in the mid-years of the 20th century to repair our aging buildings and to renovate them for ministry in the modern world. All of this took place in spite of continued financial difficulties which faced the parish. Church attendance always drops after a war, and consequently, income does too. The ethnic composition of the Slope was changing radically,

Christ Blessing Children, Tiffany Guild Room

and with it, religious affiliations and fiscal circumstances. The Depression and this consequent change put the church in a precarious situation.

A very modest endowment fund accumulated during the first part of the 1960's, amounting to roughly $13,000, which was invested in the diocesan mutual fund. In the summer of 1963 a lady, Mrs. Palen B. Nelson, who was born two blocks away on Park Place eighty-seven years before, died, leaving half her fortune to Saint John's Church, and half to Saint John's Home for the Aged. Her will was written in 1960. After the estate was settled, Saint John's received its portion of the legacy in the amount of over $400,000. This was the seed long prayed for from which Saint John's current Endowment Fund has grown. As in most other parishes, financial difficulties continue to plague the parish but it is worthwhile noting that at least since the early 1980's the vestry has been pleased to point out at Annual Parish Meetings that, though there may be some difficulty raising funds from time to time to pay regular expenses, the parish has been and remains debt free, owning no mortgage or other such financial obligations.

$15,000! The window is a delight of the beauty of art and diversity! – Fr. Powers

Tragic Crash in Park Slope

As all of this building and repair activity was going on within, a great tragedy occurred which shocked the nation and impacted our community for many years. The great tragedy struck Park Slope in 1960 only a few steps from our entrance and was reported widely around the world. In December a United Airlines jet and a TWA jet collided in mid-air over Staten Island on a dreary icy morning. The United jet made it to Brooklyn, perhaps heading for a clearing in Prospect Park. It nose-dived, however, into the Pillar of Fire Church, which was located on Sterling Place directly behind Saint John's Church.

One hundred and fifty people were killed in the crash, which destroyed the Church on Sterling Place as well as a brownstone funeral parlor and three stores. The Reverend Harry Stirling, an elderly Curate at Saint John's, was finishing an Ember Friday Mass when the explosion hit, and thought at first that the boiler had blown up. He rushed to the scene and attended in his characteristic fatherly and gentle way, the only survivor, a young boy from Illinois. The news media made much of this incident and followed it to its sad conclusion, when the lad died twenty-eight hours later. Many prayers for him and all the other victims were offered around the world and especially here at Saint John's, only a few steps from where they all died.

Born in May of 1928, while still in office as Rector, Father Clifford Buck died in July of 1985 after 28 years of faithful service to the parish.

Father Buck had been ill for many years. According to our first history book he was hospitalized with a rare blood disease for six months in 1960, only two years into his ministry here. Although he accomplished a great deal here during his ministry he was really never entirely well. He was cremated and his ashes now rest in our Memorial Garden.

Father Clifford Buck

After Father Buck's death the Bishop felt that the parish needed some time to recover from his loss and to reconsider who they were as the people of God in this place and where they wanted to go with the ministry of Christ placed in their trust. He assigned Father David Hoopes, among a few others, to serve as Interim Priest. Father Hoopes is a member of the Holy Cross religious order and later became the international Superior of that Order. He was greatly loved here at Saint John's and under his gentle leadership the parish began to heal from its loss. The Bishop also assigned a mentor to guide the parish leadership in drawing up a Parish Profile, something that seems never to have been done before in this parish. The Profile, which is still available for study, offers the following Introduction:

This profile is a brief look at Saint John's Church, Brooklyn, New York. Included are facts and viewpoints gathered for a parish self-study in the process of searching for a rector to lead our parish family. As in all families, many people participated in compiling the information, parish organizations and individual parishioners. We believe the facts are presented with accuracy. However, it is difficult to document the faith, dedication, commitment and passion for our Lord that is the hallmark of the people of Saint John's.

Under a section titled Church History is an interesting short summary of everything you have read above!:

The history of Saint John's runs parallel to that of the borough of Brooklyn. Saint John's, the second Episcopal Church established in Brooklyn, was founded in 1826, in what was then known as the

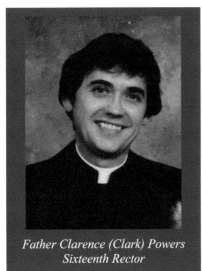

Father Clarence (Clark) Powers
Sixteenth Rector

Village of Brooklyn. The original structure was a plain wooden building located at the corner of Washington and Johnson Streets. First communion and confirmation were administered on Easter Day, April 15, 1827. As Brooklyn grew and prospered, so did Saint John's. Consequently, as the Village extended its area to the elegant area known as Park Slope, the vestry purchased several lots in Park Slope. Saint John's opened its new gothic style stone chapel in Park Slope on January 16, 1870, Saint John's Place the former Douglas Street. The chapel and nave as seen now was added in 1885. For several years Saint John's and its accompanying rectory, sat literally in the field while the city built around it.

The last sentence of that short history is what really attracted the attention of the current rector:

Saint John's Church is committed to meet the challenges of the present and the future with the same faith that has been the legacy of our past.

It goes on to describes Park Slope as *"the Victorian era at its height"* which is still true today.

The houses in Park Slope are primarily Victorian row houses, with the smaller brick buildings towards Fourth Avenue, with a few frame houses and some mansions, all built about the late 1900's. A portion of the area, Park Place to Ninth Street from Sixth Avenue to the park was designated as a New York City Landmarks District in 1973. Several other landmark areas such as Prospect Park, the Brooklyn Botanic Garden, the Brooklyn Museum, Grand Army Branch of the Brooklyn Public Library, the Grand Army Plaza and the Soldiers' and Sailors' Memorial Arch are in close proximity.

By 1986 when the Profile was being published the neighborhood was becoming rapidly *'gentrified'*, as Upwardly mobile young professionals bought up much of the existing housing stock of brownstones and converted them from single family homes or rooming houses, as many had become in the late 1950's and 1960's, to apartments and cooperatives. It states that the total population of Park Slope was 54,944 and says that the population has decreased due to the renovations of the housing stock.[35] This seems to be a continuing trend as the latest population figures indicate that the population is now 39,787 with a density of 44,105 people per square mile. The neighborhood was racially inclusive:

> *Although whites predominate,(61%), the population includes 24.2% Hispanics and 15.6% Blacks. The most noticeable racial population shift occurred in the 1960's when a combination of public policy and the need for land space led to the out migration of substantial numbers of middle-class whites out of Brooklyn to suburbia. With the out migration of whites, and the revised immigration laws, blacks from Harlem, the South and Central Americas, Africa and the West Indies settled in Park Slope. However, population migration between 1970 and 1980 reveals a reversing trend, with whites continuing to move into the area at a considerably higher rate than blacks.*

This observation was correct since current data indicates that the neighborhood today is about 87% white but it still maintains a rich racial and ethnic diversity within its own borders and in neighboring areas.[36]

One of the most interesting portions of the profile is the goals at the end and the description of the sort of priest they hoped to find.

> *It is hoped that after the rector has completed one year that St. John's Church will have increased membership. ... We hope that together we will strive to maintain the existing buildings and still have a budget surplus. Through the delivery of inspiring sermons we look for guidance in developing a richer spiritual life. After the rector has been with us for five years, we hope to have a thriving youth and outreach ministry and organized programs for the elderly. In addition to financial stability we will commit*

[35] *The area known as Park Slope today is a much larger geographic area than it was in 1980 since real estate developers have pushed its boundaries into adjoining neighborhoods to take advantage of the more desirable reputation of the "Slope" and increase housing costs.*

[36] http://www.city-data.com/neighborhood/Park-Slope-Brooklyn-NY.html

ourselves to stewardship of time, talent and tithing, Within ten years our new rector should implement plans to meet the needs for additional space, senior citizens housing, and the formation of an elementary Episcopal school. We hope to have increased activities for all ages and fulfillment of all our previous goals.

A survey of the parish indicates that the most important criteria for most people were that the Rector be talented in the following areas:

1. Preacher
2. Theologian
3. Administrative Leader
4. Crisis Minister
5. Spiritual Guide/Leader
6. Youth Worker/Teacher

We hope our new rector will be a caring administrator, possessing zeal and passion for our Lord that has been a legacy of the people of St. John's Church.

After interviewing a number of candidates the Reverend Clarence H. Powers was elected Rector and took up his duties on February 1st, 1987. Father Powers was born in Memphis, Tennessee, graduated from Memphis State University and served in the Army during the Vietnam War as a French Linguist in the Army Security Agency. He completed his studies for ministry at General Theological Seminary in New York and was ordained Priest at Christ Church, Nashville, in 1977. His first assignment as priest was to become Vicar of Saint James Church, Dickson County, Tennessee, where he served for just over three years.

Saint James had been closed for about 65 years when the Bishop assigned him the task of opening it up again in 1977. Just west of Nashville, Dickson County was a high growth area at the time as several important companies moved south to benefit from lower costs in wages, property taxes and heating costs. St. James was the only Episcopal parish in the county and the Bishop offered Father Powers a three-year contract to go there, open the church and build a congregation. It was quite a challenge but when he left the parish had about 100 members, a youth group, Sunday School and several services during the week as well as on Sunday. Property had been purchased on which a new church building was to be built.

Realizing that if he stayed any longer he would be caught up in a major building project that would last for several years, he decided it was time to move on and accepted a position in New York as the part-time editor of the *Ecumenical Bulletin* published by the Episcopal Church at its headquarters at 815 Second Avenue. He also began studies at General Theological and later at New York University towards a doctorate in Christian Education.

A few months after he arrived in New York he was assigned Priest in Charge of St. Stephen and St. Martin's Church in Bedford Stuyvesant, Brooklyn. Being more interested in parish ministry than either publishing or his studies he accepted the call to become Rector of that parish in 1981 and served there until he was called to Saint John's where he took up his duties as Rector on February 1, 1987.

Father Powers receiving a Prayer Book at his Institution in May, 1987

Preparing for the New Millennium

The way people lived and the way the Church ministered to them changed very slowly for thousands of years. A farmer from 14th-century England would have not think life so very different if he were to somehow find himself in the same country 200 years later. But the pace of change moved much more rapidly after the Industrial Age expanded throughout the western world in the 19th century.

By the end of the 20th century something many began to call the Information Age helped to hasten the pace of change even more as, first TV and then computers, revolutionized the way we all lived our lives and perceived the world around us. But as is often the case in parishes, change was slow coming to Saint John's.

CHAPTER SEVEN: OFFICES, EQUIPMENT AND PEOPLE WHO USE THEM

When Father Powers arrived at Saint John's the only office space available was a small room in the basement of the Rectory. That office was equipped with a typewriter and a rather ancient copy machine. The week before he moved into the Rectory it was broken into and robbed. The typewriter was stolen, but that didn't matter a great deal since the secretary could not type!

The new Rector was already computer literate, something quite rare in 1987, and he brought his own portable computer with him. He had purchased it with his own funds in 1984 while Rector of Saint Stephen and Saint Martin's Church. There were no funds at that parish to hire a secretary and he realized that he could spend less time preparing the bulletins each week and more easily communicate to members of the parish through mailings if he learned to use computers and database programs. So he taught himself and then began to teach others to use word processing programs, spreadsheets and databases.

After a few months in office at Saint John's he convinced the parish leadership to acquire a more up-to-date computer and to hire a full-time secretary to use it. At the time there was a wonderful program offered through the public school system in New York which placed recent graduates into offices like ours so that they could gain experience to help get a better job after a couple of years. We were very fortunate to hire a young lady named Daisy Jimenez who was very skilled in the use of computers. Daisy helped us create major databases of parish members and their families including birth, baptismal and confirmation dates, and much more. Birthday letters, quarterly giving reports, and other such things began to be sent to members on a regular basis. In time other databases were created for all baptismal, marriage, confirmation, and burial records of the parish from 1826 to date. Work still continues on these important databases, but they have proved invaluable many times over in saving time in searching parish historical records quickly and easily while allowing the old books to be stored safely in a fire-proof safe.

As the office equipment expanded to include computers, a new copy machine and fax machines, more space was needed. A portion of the undercroft was sectioned off where two new offices were constructed, one for the Rector and another for the secretary. Daisy worked with us for about two years and with the work experience she then had on her resume, was able to get a job in a business office in Manhattan.

Several months were spent interviewing new people for the job but no one was found to fill Daisy's shoes until one of our own members retired from her position as private secretary to a Federal Judge. Sheila Mackie, who had worked for 40 or so years in law offices, came to the Rector and asked about the position. She had a wonderful retirement income including full medical insurance, so she was not concerned about the salary. Rather, she wanted to work a few days a less week and wanted new office equipment. Father Powers was delighted and said he would welcome her help in the office but had no funds for new equipment. Sheila said

Sheila Mackie
Parish Secretary 1991 - 2010

that was not a problem, she would buy everything herself! The next day she and the Rector took a cab to J and R Computer World and bought everything needed!

Sheila worked here for 15 years until she moved to North Carolina to be near her daughter and grandchildren. She was greatly loved in the parish and it was very difficult to find someone to replace her. Several wonderful volunteers jumped in to help, especially Janet Hibbert who had worked on and off for years with Sheila as a volunteer. Several other paid employees have filled the position for a short periods of time before pursuing other careers. Lately, we have been very fortunate to have a young man who has become our Parish Administrator. A recent college graduate, James Olszewski hopes to go to Seminary soon to study for the priesthood and will work with us until that happens.

The Parish Profile hoped that attendance and membership would grow as the new Rector took charge of the congregation and it did. Once the computer system was up and running the Rector sent a letter to all members of the parish who had not been seen in church for months, or in some cases years, telling them that they would be marked "Inactive" on the next Parochial Report unless they came to church more regularly. As you can imagine, this resulted in a lot of "rumpled feathers", but quite a few people made sure that they at least attended a bit more regularly.

CHAPTER EIGHT: CHURCH GROWTH IN NUMBERS AND SPIRIT

But a real problem with Church Growth identified by the Rector and parish leadership was a lack of visibility in the neighborhood, both literally and figuratively. Unlike most of the other major churches in Park Slope, Saint John's is not located on the frequently traveled avenues, but rather on a quiet side street. It was also not very well lit and mostly was hidden behind some rather large trees. Many people walked right past it or within a few feet of it and had no idea that a church was there. This was verified by the parish leadership who went out into the neighborhood and asked passersby if they could direct them to St. John's Episcopal Church. Almost no one could do so.

The trees in the garden were trimmed back so that the major church sign became more visible. Another large Episcopal Church sign was acquired to be displayed on an inner fence. Thanks to a rather large donation from a young advertising executive named Bruce Goerlich who served on our vestry, we were able to hire lighting experts who designed and installed flood lights to shine on the bellcote so that it became a visible symbol to anyone walking on St. John's Place and to those crossing the street at Seventh Avenue. And to be sure that we were heard as well as seen, a special offering was taken up to install an electronic carillon to ring out the hour and half hours between 9 AM and 9 PM each day and to play hymns at noon and 6 PM.

As the parish became more physically visible in the neighborhood it also became more figuratively visible as it welcomed all sorts of community groups to make use of its space for important gatherings and opportunities for fellowship and art. Groups meeting here have included block associations, handgun control groups, AA, Al-Anon, Narcotics Anonymous, Girl Scouts, theater groups, and many others. In time, most people in the neighborhood knew that Saint John's was open and actively involved in the life of the community.

But the Rector and leadership were also concerned for those in need around us. So, in 1988 an Outreach Committee, called the Social Concerns Committee, was formed to participate with other churches and nonprofit groups in identifying and meeting the needs of people within the community. This group has served ever since then as the catalyst for an organized outreach ministry effort to serve the needs of people with AIDS, to gather food and clothing for the poor, toys and gifts for the needy at Christmas and much more. Joining with other churches, Saint John's is a major supporter of Christian Help in Park Slope, CHIPS, our local soup kitchen located nearby on Fourth Avenue. In addition to gathering food contributions each week, every year Saint John's leads a major effort to supply cooked turkeys and all the ingredients for a wonderful Thanksgiving Day meal for the homeless and the elderly in the community.

As a result of the ministry of this committee within the parish, Father Powers was asked to be on the board of the group concerned with the plight of mother's in prison, centered at nearby Gethsemane Presbyterian Church. He worked with that ministry for a number of years and led Saint John's each year in gathering toys and other gifts to present to incarcerated mothers so that they could offer their children a gift on Christmas Day.

In the late 1980's many people were dying from the opportunistic diseases that accompany AIDS. Some of them were abandoned by their families and were living and suffering alone. Some of these died and were cremated and buried here in our garden. Others came here to worship and to seek support. Father Powers joined with others to form the Brooklyn Episcopal AIDS Committee in 1989. It was the first such organization within the Diocese of Long Island so participants represented not only Brooklyn, but also the Diocese of Long Island at national and regional meetings seeking support for people living with AIDS. That group operated from Saint John's for several years until the Diocese of Long Island created its own Diocesan AIDS Commission.

Another first for Saint John's and for the Archdeaconry of Brooklyn was the Archdeaconry Website created by Father Powers at the request of Archdeacon Peter Golden. As with the earlier Brooklyn Episcopal AIDS Committee, it also stood alone for several years as the only website other than local parish sites in the Diocese. Since the Bishop's Office had no email address and the Diocese had no website, email that should have been directed to their offices in Garden City arrived in our email box here at Saint John's. For several years Father Powers forwarded all of this mail as best he could to the phone numbers of the proper recipients.

Saint John's own website was developed by Father Powers in 1996. At first it was a rather simple site hosted by the National Council of Churches. This organization provided free web-space and easy-to-use templates so that all churches could have an online presence. As he began to use the site to communicate parish schedules and activities, Father Powers realized that a great tool for ministry was being developed and most of his colleagues didn't know anything about it.

This led him to seek a grant from the Lilly Foundation in 2001 that he used to finance a Sabbatical spent at the Episcopal Divinity School of the Pacific in Berkeley, California, where he studied Web Site Development and Internet Ministry. When he returned to Brooklyn he was appointed Dean of Saint John's Deanery, then a collection of eight churches in central Brooklyn. Working with Archdeacon Peter Golden, his position as Dean required extra responsibilities but no extra salary!

His basic responsibilities as Dean were twofold, to assist parishes in Brooklyn to develop Internet ministry and to organize educational programs for the Archdeaconry. This ministry expanded later as he also helped develop a Computer Lab at the Mercer School of Theology where he taught lay people from parishes around the Diocese to set up and maintain websites for their own parishes.

His second area of responsibility included setting up Confirmation Classes and Lenten Programs for the Archdeaconry. Various priests were asked to teach particular subjects for the Confirmation Classes, which were designed to augment such classes offered in each parish. Seminary Professors and other noted educators were engaged to teach Lenten Programs each year. These classes were quite popular and included instructors from General Theological Seminary and Princeton as well as many others. Some people remarked that the thing they liked the best about these classes was that it allowed them to meet other Episcopalians in Brooklyn and to get to see other Episcopal Parishes, since they were hosted at different churches each week.

During this time a number of people came to speak with the Rector about exploring the possibility of studying for Holy Orders. Any time that someone in a congregation feels called to consider serving God and the church as an ordained minister it is usually an indication that spirituality has been strongly nourished in that place. So the Parish Profile quoted above that hoped *for guidance in developing a richer spiritual life* seems to have become a reality!

In the past quarter century the worship, educational opportunities and the spirituality that these things have enhanced have caused three people to explore their vocations and then to study and become ordained as priests in the Episcopal Church. Others may have done the same thing in prior years but if so there is currently no record of it. The most recent of these three we have already heard a bit about. Father Luke Fodor and his wife Willow have both been very active in the ministry we have offered in the past few years. Luke is from Ohio and Willow is from Washington State. They met while attending school in Chicago, Illinois. Later they married

Father Luke Fodor preaching and Mother Kristin Kopren celebrating the Mass at Saint John's

and moved to England where Luke received a Masters Degree in Theology at Durham University. They moved to Park Slope the following year where they lived while he pursued another Masters Degree in Philosophy at New York University and Willow taught English.

Although they had attended Anglican Churches in England they had been raised in non-denominational Community Churches. Shortly after coming to Saint John's they joined the Confirmation Class and became Confirmed Episcopalians. They each also became Licensed Eucharistic Ministers, thurifers, and members of the vestry as well as directors of our Youth Program. About the only thing they didn't do was sing in the choir, and neither of them felt called to do that!

In time Luke entered the ordination process by becoming sponsored first by Saint John's and then by the Bishop and Diocese of Long Island. He studied at Bexley Hall Seminary in Ohio and was ordained Deacon here at Saint John's in February of 2011 and then Priest at Saint John's Church in Cold Spring Harbor where he now works.

Paul Hartt came to one of the groups meeting here at Saint John's on Thursday evenings and a short time later began coming to the mass which was offered just before that meeting. He was the son of an Episcopal Priest and had thought long and hard about whether he himself really had a vocation. When he felt that he had he came and spoke with the Rector about it and then began the process which led to his study at Yale Divinity School and ordination to the priesthood. He now serves as Rector of St. Peter's Church in the Diocese of Albany.

Mother Kristin Kopren moved to Park Slope from North Carolina in 1989 to work at Newsweek magazine. Though she had been raised in a

Father Paul Hartt

somewhat conservative southern denomination, she was intrigued by a Healing Mass offered one Thursday evening and came to the service. She stayed for a bit of fellowship afterwards and joined the Confirmation Class. Later she became the editor of our monthly Newsletter, a member of the vestry and a Licensed Eucharistic Minister. She married her husband Tom here at Saint John's and attended General Theological Seminary in Manhattan. After ordination she served parishes in Manhattan and, for the past 10 years or so, has served as the Chaplain at Saint Hilda and Saint Hugh's School operated by the Episcopal Sisters of the Holy Spirit.

We thank God for the life and witness among us of these people from Saint John's and pray for the continued success of their ministry and for the continued spiritual life here which nourished them.

In 1992 the Rector and vestry moved at long last to address the often expressed need for classroom and meeting spaces which had plagued the parish for more than 100 years. A fire severely damaged a brownstone building on Seventh Avenue adjacent to the church property. Because it was fire damaged the building was available for a much lower price than it would have been otherwise. It was purchased for $325,000, much below market value. But it presented the parish with a major challenge which it was just not ready to meet.

Several members of the congregation decided that the Rector and vestry had acted unwisely in making the purchase of a building which needed so many repairs. In hindsight they were probably correct, though their vocal and strident opposition did not help matters at all, but rather made things much worse. In a very short time they translated their dissatisfaction with an investment into opposition to virtually everything the Rector and parish leadership tried to do. They created so much tension that visitors didn't return and several longtime members stopped coming to church.

It was exactly the sort of thing that happened shortly after the death of Father Guion as we saw earlier in this book. At that time there was such violent disagreement among the leadership that most of the vestry resigned and it was very difficult to replace them. Several clergy were called to become Rector but all declined upon seeing the internal dissension of the congregation causing Bishop Potter to step in to encourage Father Seymour to reconsider his rejection of the post of Rector and to come "to lead a forlorn hope" in recovering the parish of Saint John's, Brooklyn, New York, from the distressing condition into which internal dissension had brought it.

Like Father Guion before him, Father Buck died in office leaving many people to grieve. When what came to be called the Parish House was purchased the Rector was still so new to the parish that many still called him Father Buck! It would no doubt have been best not to make such a major financial investment so early in his term of office. But it was the sort of thing Father Powers did in his ministry. He led his first parish in growth and then purchased land where a new church was to be built. His second parish, in Brooklyn, had been allowed to badly deteriorate before he became Rector, but within six years he had installed new windows, new siding and built a new office. In both of those cases, the laity were solid in their support with growth in numbers and expansion of the parish plant. It was not so at Saint John's so soon after the death of Father Buck.

The dissension was caused by a small but very vocal group of very unpleasant people (yes, such people are often to be found even in the best of parishes! In recent years several books have been written on power struggles in parishes, including one book graphically entitled *Clergy Killers*!). But unlike the earlier dissension after the death of Father Guion, there was a Rector in office and he and the vestry were not divided. The leadership continued to work together in the best interest of the people of the parish and those who tried to undermine them eventually left. But the damage they inflicted ensured that the Parish House would never be completed.

But we made good use of that building for about 10 years. Adjacent to the church itself, it was part of the original Saint John's Church property which was sold during financial difficulties in the latter part of the 19th century. Heating and lighting were restored to the building and the vestry approved spending about $75,000 to renovate it as best we could with those funds available.

The parlor floor had a front and a rear parlor which were converted into a choir rehearsal room also available as a meeting room with a separate Music Office behind it. The ground floor and the 4th floors provided space for six Sunday School classrooms. The 3rd floor became an apartment for the sexton and the top floor, a sort of vast loft space, became headquarters for our teen ministry and was also used for rehearsal space by several theater groups and for dance classes. Later the ground floor was converted into an apartment for our Assistant Priest.

In a leap of faith the vestry voted funds to hire a professional Director of Christian Education. Mother Angela Askew, who had taught at New

York Theological Seminary and who had served as a non-stipendiary assistant at Saint John's for several years, was hired and began a wonderful ministry of education for the whole parish. Introducing a course of study called Faith Care, she assembled a volunteer staff of 10 or 12 teachers and the Sunday School grew in size and scope for several years. Her vision was not just education for the Sunday School but for the whole parish. A wide variety of programs of study were offered for all and the enthusiasm was felt in all aspects of parish life. But even with new growth the parish was never able to raise the funds to sustain the added costs to the budget. After about five years of heavy deficit spending the educational program was abandoned, the Director of Christian Education was let go and the building was put up for sale.

In 2003 the building on Seventh Avenue was sold for just over $1 million, almost three times the purchase price. The Endowment Fund was replenished and funds were made available for long-needed repairs and renovations to the church and Rectory buildings, but sadly the dream of a strong ministry of education and space to house it were once again allowed to die. Since the move to Park Slope and the loss of the mysterious Sunday School building at the old location, mentioned earlier, classes for children and adults had to meet in whatever corners could be found in the church and undercroft. They still do today.

But some good things came out of that 10-year investment in money and energy. Many children and adults received quality education in those years, community groups were housed and allowed to flourish, and eventually a great financial profit was realized. So, as in the case so often in God's ministry when new things are tried and fail, much good also came out of it all.

Making use of some of the funds received from the sale the vestry set aside $200,000 to carry out a number of projects in a campaign called *Making Old Things New*. Asbestos was removed from both the church and Rectory buildings at a cost of $24,000. A new boiler replaced one that had become dangerous in the Rectory for a total cost of $5,500. The old sound system in the church was replaced with excellent modern equipment for around $15,000. Air conditioning was installed in the church for another $15,000.

As is often the case, one of the most expensive items in this campaign, though necessary for the health of the building had very little impact on the life and ministry of the parish. The repair of the Rectory gutters cost more than $75,000, more than everything else combined! Since the Rectory is a landmark building in a landmark neighborhood, these gutters and the woodwork that held them up had to be recreated exactly as they had been originally. So scaffolding was put up and the work began. But it was constantly delayed during one of the worse winters experienced for years adding to the cost.

The balance was used, along with some donations from parishioners, to renovate the parish gardens and kitchen.

CHAPTER NINE: RENOVATING THE PARISH GARDENS

Sadly, in today's world most churches in large cities are locked up most of the time for security reasons, but people still need quiet and peaceful places to come and pray, meditate or just sit peacefully. So what can churches do to protect themselves from vandalism and theft but still be available to meet the needs of the people in the neighborhood it is supposed to serve? The Rector and leadership of Saint John's decided that the church's front yard should be renovated into three inviting spaces.

The first of these, nearest the rectory, has become a space set with attractive plants, walks and benches where people can sit and pray or meditate. It is called the Memorial Garden since it is the place where the ashes of more than 20 people (and at least two dogs) have been buried over the years.

Another longer garden was laid out with new plantings, walks and benches where people can sit individually or in small groups for quiet reading or conversations. This is called our Meditation Garden and it has a small plaque beneath the statue of an angel dedicating it to Ruth Beck[37]

---

[37] *Henry McCadden, from the local funeral home, called the Rector late one afternoon in 1989 to say that he had a couple in his office who wanted to pre-plan their funerals and that they would like to have them at Saint John's Church. They were both in their 80's*

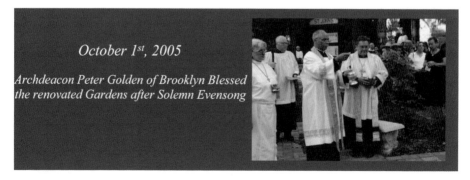

October 1st, 2005

Archdeacon Peter Golden of Brooklyn Blessed the renovated Gardens after Solemn Evensong

Students first removed most plants and leveled the ground. Then they dug walkways 6 inches deep and filled in with a layer of gravel and another of sand. Then they set in the stones and leveled them. Plants and bushes were then replanted and others were added. All this took about 4 months, from June - September of 2005.

who left a generous donation to the parish shortly before the garden was renovated.

The third area is a concreted space directly in front of the building. Originally this was concreted to keep water from seeping into the basement but little was done to beautify or utilize the space. Susan Maldovan drew up a plan for it to become a wonderful community space with tables, umbrellas, and large pots of plants and bushes. On Sundays in nice weather

and had been married at Saint Bartholomew's Episcopal Church in Brooklyn many years before when that parish was the height of High Society but but had not attended church anywhere for many years. Plans were made and a few years later the husband died and the funeral was held as planned. Soon after that the widow's maid called the office to invite the Rector to Tea but when asked if she would like to receive he was told not to bother, that she just wanted to chat for a bit since she was an invalid and not able to get out and about. The invitations to Tea came fairly regularly every few months until her own death a few years later. Her funeral was held here and she left the parish about $50,000. She hardly ever took communion but often said how much she loved the liturgy of the Episcopal Church.

Garden before renovation, above, Garden after renovation below.

this provides a wonderful space for Iced Tea after Mass. Throughout the week neighbors often bring lunch and share it in the peace of the garden. It has become quite a popular spot in the neighborhood and the parish is happy to have everyone use it.

The new patio area in the front garden is now used for Iced Tea Hour after Mass in nice weather

But when this project was proposed in 2005 most of the funds that had been set aside for renovations had been spent. Mr. Keith Davenport, a landscape architect who had already designed and built a beautiful garden for the nearby Brooklyn Conservatory of Music, volunteered to design plans for Saint John's Garden. His design would have cleared the entire garden of all trees and shrubs, then more soil would be brought in to build it up with retaining walls all around the boundaries, and then new plants would be put in along with paths and benches. The cost to do all this was about $50,000!

Needless to say, this was far more money than was available, but something clearly had to be done. So the Rector called for volunteers to help plan and build a new garden. The architect kindly gave us his plans and told us we could rework them however we wanted. We set to work.

Sally Brodsky, our Senior Warden at the time, had experience as a set designer for theater. So she drew plans for us based upon what we already had. Her plans did not require completely clearing the garden but did call for the removal of two tall trees on either side of the Chapel entrance which had come to effectively hide that entrance and the bellcote. A very large bush which also hid the main entrance was removed. Walks and bench sites were laid out, then dug and installed by a band of college students hired and directed by the Rector and volunteers. Chief among these were Luke and Willow Fodor and the parish Youth Group.[38]

---

[38] *We had to remove two trees as we cleared the garden so Luke Fodor, raised in a rural area of Ohio, climbed up to the top of each with a chain saw and set to work as his wife and the Rector prayed below!*

The Memorial Garden

The Episcopal Church Women raised several thousand dollars which the vestry matched from the ***Making Old Things New Fund*** for a total of $8500 and the garden was built over the summer of 2005. Of course, a garden is a growing, living thing so it is never finished! As so often happens in ministry, when a need becomes apparent God often sends someone to meet it. And so it was at Saint John's.

Susan Maldovan, who had long lived in an apartment in Manhattan moved around the corner to a garden apartment. Susan didn't know much about gardening at the time but wanted to do something with her backyard so she took a course at the nearby Brooklyn Botanic Garden. Her interest grew and soon she volunteered to take care of our garden here and has done a magnificent job as everyone in the neighborhood will attest! The Archdeacon of Brooklyn came to bless the garden after a service of Solemn Evensong on October 2, 2005, the first of many gala Garden Parties that followed!

CHAPTER TEN: RENOVATING THE PARISH KITCHEN

Food and fellowship have been a part of most of the things done at Saint John's during its long history. By 2007 the parish kitchen, which had been installed some 70 or so years before was in bad shape. The floor was rotten in places and the stove was an impossible old iron monstrosity that would have been at home in the Victorian era. In short, it was dark, dirty and very inconvenient.

A drive for funds yielded about $30,000 and the vestry added what was left in the *Making Old Things New* Fund (about $25,000 or so) to redevelop the kitchen into a new, light, clean and modern space. Once again Senior Warden Sally Brodsky drew up plans and an Irish company called New Tech was hired to do the work. They were fantastically talented workmen who took everything out, gutted the space, installed new flooring, new ceiling, new electricity and new appliances. Since we did not have the money for new cabinets, they completely rebuilt the ones we already had

Before and after renovations

into beautiful and useful new storage units with new counters.

The job began in June of 2007 and finished up shortly before Thanksgiving of that year. The Rector said at the time that the two most important spaces in most parishes were first the altar and then the kitchen! Evidently most of the parish agreed with him since they gave sacrificially to create this new and useful space!

Lay Ministry

As we come near to the end of this book it might be helpful to take another look at the way it began. In the Preface, ministry in the *Book of Common Prayer* is described this way: *the ministers of the church are lay persons, bishops, priests, and deacons.* But so far this book has primarily been a description of the Rectors of this parish and what was done while they were in office. That is not what I wanted to do, but it was the only thing that could be done with the resource materials available from vestry minutes and newspaper articles. These documents seldom tell about ministries of the laity who have offered time and talent as Sunday School teachers, choristers, ushers, and Altar Guild volunteers. Countless others have organized drives for clothing and food to serve those in need or visited the sick. The names of all of these people and so many more are not found in vestry minutes or in newspaper accounts, even though it they who breathed the breath of life into the ministry of the parish.

But tI have been Rector of this parish for over a quarter of a century. So as we come to the end of Our Story a bit of the story that they and I created together so that others who come after us will remember them as well as me.

TEACHERS

Education programs at Saint John's never really recuperated from loss of classroom space and professional educational staff after the sale of the Parish House. Students were disappointed and several teachers left the parish. But a few very talented and committed people have worked hard to maintain some viable educational opportunities for children on Sunday mornings, a vital program for teens and opportunities for adult education.

Almost single-handedly for several years a dedicated teacher named Charmaine Jacob has kept Sunday School alive for early elementary students. Meeting in the undercroft at 11 AM, the class is mainly made up of children from pre-school through 5th or 6th grade. Charmaine has attracted a number of people who have helped over the past few years, especially from our teenagers. Usually one of the lessons assigned for the Sunday Readings is introduced to the children in an age appropriate manner and they are encouraged to do small projects to enhance learning. After about 45 minutes they join the rest of the congregation in time to receive a blessing or communion.

In addition to these regular classes, Sunday School sponsors a Christmas Party every year with a visit from St. Nicholas, who brings a gift for each child, and *The Great*

Charmaine Jacob

All-American Easter Egg Hunt on the Sunday following Easter. Other activities sponsored for the kids have included Christmas Pageants and Christmas *Tableau Vivant,* Halloween parties and many other fun activities. Charmaine and those who have worked with her have offered a solid foundation of Christian education for our children and a great deal of fun! Perhaps the way most of the children feel about the program can be summed up in a exclamation so loud it was overheard by everyone in the church a year or so ago. As the children were coming up the staircase from the undercroft to the sanctuary, 5 year-old Phillip Hunter was heard to exclaim, *"I REALLY LOVE THIS PLACE!"*

The Parish House had provided us with a large sort of loft room on the top floor that became a headquarters for our Teen Ministry. Our Christian Education Director had a partner named Alex who studied Youth Ministry and offered that here at Saint John's as part of her learning experience. She was very talented and in time attracted a large host of teens to a series of classes and parties. Many of the teens were unchurched and got their first glimpse of organized religion here at Saint John's. With the sale of the Parish House that program came to an end as well, but a vital teen ministry has continued to be offered over the years by a series of volunteers including two of whom went on to become Episcopal Priests, Luke Fodor and Rob Picken, and Doug Hecklinger who serves as a New York City public school teacher.

As the parish adjusted to the loss of its professional educational staff, Luke and Willow Fodor managed to revive what had become a somewhat floundering youth program. They met regularly with the young people and helped them develop into a cohesive group that shared discussions and trips to nearby places of interest. A seminarian from General Theological

Seminary named Rob Picken was only here for a year working with Luke and Willow and the group but became greatly loved and respected during that time by all. He now serves as the Liturgical Officer of the Diocese of Long Island.

Doug Hecklinger and his partner Kyle moved to Park Slope about 4 years ago. Doug is a fifth grade teacher and Kyle works for Mayor Bloomberg. They met while in college in Washington, DC. Doug grew up in the Episcopal Church and strongly believes that everyone in the parish should be involved in

Doug Hecklinger

the education and nurturing of our children. Parents of our teens are very grateful for the work he has done with their children. Perhaps the greatest compliment he has received has been from some of the teens who say *Doug is the Man!*

Led by these talented people and lots of others who have joined to help with special trips and projects, the teens have worked hard to learn how to live Christian lives in a rapidly changing world. They meet every Sunday at 11 AM to discuss the Sunday readings and then join the congregation for Communion. Many of them also serve as acolytes.

Adult education has not been neglected either in the past few years. Bible Study and other educational opportunities are offered frequently here at Saint John's by the Rector, visiting priests and scholars and lots of lay people. Lenten programs of study are offered each year and have always been fairly well attended. These classes usually begin the week after Ash Wednesday and conclude the week before Holy Week. Confirmation classes are usually offered for several weeks after Easter and Bible Study classes are offered at various times in the year.

Dr. Juliet Emanuel-George has always been a strong supporter of the education programs at Saint John's Church. Juliet was

Dr. Juliet Emanuel-George

born in Guyana, South America. She is married to Patrick George, brother to the retired Anglican Bishop of that country. One of the first Lenten Programs offered by Father Powers when he became Rector featured classes taught by Bishop George, arranged by Juliet. She has earned her PhD in English and is a professor at Borough of Manhattan Community College. Recently, she has also become the first woman Executive Director of College English Association.

Juliet hosted one of the most popular gatherings for authors that we have ever had, called *The Literary Hang*. It is an annual event hosted by a Guyanese Cultural Association that welcomes the participation of everyone interested in writing. In the course of a Sunday afternoon neighbors and passersby joined in to swell the numbers of participants until the garden literally overflowed!

Committed to her faith and her Church, Juliet received the Bishop's Cross Award from the Bishop of Long Island for outstanding service in ministry. She has served in many capacities at Saint John's but, in addition to her educational endeavors, is perhaps best known here at Saint John's for her hospitality as Chair of our Fellowship Committee and her strong leadership as Senior Warden.[39]

Cate Pegram spent several years teaching Sunday School and then as Director of Education before she married and moved to Paris. Tony Foglia was a talented teacher for several years before he moved to Tacoma, Washington. Lee Willis began a wonderful Book Club a few years ago that encouraged many people to read and become more involved in the life of the parish. Ellen Murphy and Susan McHenry taught Bible Study on Sundays for adults. Bob Hayes began a Prayer and Praise group that encouraged both of those things. There are so many others who have helped with the Educational Ministry at Saint John's in recent years that they cannot

---

[39] *In 1994 New York City was beset by a series of incredible thunder storms which dumped huge amounts of water on the city within a few minutes time. The Undercroft and the offices located on that level flooded often as the drains overflowed. One evening six or more inches of water filled the Undercroft and more was cascading down the steps from the utility room just outside the Guild Room. The sink in that room had become a geyser, shooting water high into the air. Junior Warden Curtis Chase was trying to stem the tide by stuffing rags into the drain and holding them down with a heavy fire extinguisher. But the water still splashed up and over the nearby electric panel. I jumped in to help Curtis fight the geyser. We struggled for a bit until Juliet appeared at the foot of the staircase dressed in Wellington boots and shouting for us to get out! She then ran and did the sensible thing that neither of us had thought to do, she threw the main electric switch turning off the power. Thank God for Juliet!*

all be named here. But their contributions have all been appreciated by those they have taught and whose lives they have influenced.

MUSICIANS

After serving the congregation faithfully for 38 years as Music Director, Mr. John Brian McAnuff retired in January of 2009. He had maintained and practically rebuilt the organ during those 38 years and had produced a music program widely known as one of the best in Brooklyn. In addition to directing the choir and playing the organ on Sunday, for many years Brian offered wonderful concerts throughout the year and was especially noted for conducting inspired musical programs at Easter and Christmas featuring a small orchestra as well as the organ.

A respected composer, he wrote and arranged many anthems and settings of the liturgy, a number of which are still sung regularly here at Saint John's and other places. Several of these compositions were published by the Oxford University Press, including *This Is the Truth, I will Lift Up Mine Eyes,* and his well-known and beloved arrangement of *Swing Low, Sweet Chariot.*

Prior to his retirement, Brian had been hospitalized a number of times, for cancer treatment in his last few years of service. His bones had become very brittle due to radiation therapy and, after a terrible fall in which his shoulder was broken, he had to retire. A gala retirement party was given

*Above, Brian McAnuff
directing the choir, 1971
Left, Palm Sunday 2004
Wearing the Bishop's Cross*

for him and he moved with his partner, Bayard Buckley, to Fort Myers, Florida, to be near his sister.

Mr. Cryder Bankes, a librarian at CBS News and a respected musician who had served for Brian during much of the time he was ill, became the new Music Director in 2009. He set about building up the volunteer choir which had declined greatly in the last years of Brian's illness. Four professional section leaders were still hired to maintain our program but were joined within a few months by 8 to 10 enthusiastic volunteers.

Cryder has continued the tradition of offering concerts and musical programs and even expanded the repertoire quite a bit! One favorite activity that he began was an occasional Hymn Sing, where people are invited to come and enjoy an evening of singing hymns and sharing wine and food. The first year he was in office here he had not had much time to gather a choir or to rehearse them for a concert so he invited a number of people in the community who were not members but who liked to play instruments and sing, to come and do that here one afternoon. It was billed as *Not Your Usual Church Concert, Concert* and was so popular people are still asking us to do another one.

We haven't done that yet but last winter he worked with the Brooklyn Conservatory of Music to offer a Sing Along Messiah here to raise funds for the local soup kitchen. We also have begun hosting a series of concerts featuring talented young adult performers on Sunday afternoons called **Concerts on the Slope.** Meanwhile, the choir has grown to include 10 or so volunteers from the congregation who have become a very active and dynamic group!

WORSHIP, FELLOWSHIP, OUTREACH AND EVANGELISM

An elderly woman named Louise who had

Left, Cryder Bankes above Cryder directing the Choir at Easter 2010

served as the Altar Guild Directress for many years at Saint Stephen and Saint Martin's Church used to say to me that she never left the church until she saw the altar smiling at her. I liked that and I liked her. She was a devoted caretaker of the sacred vestments and vessels used in the Sacraments as have been most of the members of Altar Guilds I have served with throughout my 35 years as a Priest. When I came to Saint John's Church the Altar Guild was led by Pat Pegram who had held that position for many years.

Patty was born and raised in Pennsylvania where she literally married the boy next door, her husband John. He is a patent attorney and she could be described as a professional volunteer! She has been a good example to her children, teaching them that work that needs to be done does not always require payment. Throughout her life she has volunteered at schools, libraries, museums and here at Saint John's. She resigned the chair of the Altar Guild about 20 years ago but continues to help out often as needed and currently serves as Church Warden.

Florence (Joy) Parkins has directed the Guild for the past 20 years or so. Like Patty she is a strong leader who knows about all there is to know about caring for the sacred items in her charge and teaches those who work with her how to keep them in good repair. Over the years so many wonderful people have served with these two ladies and they all deserve to be mentioned if there were only room to do so!

As a soldier I used to hear it said that armies moved on their stomachs, in other words, if you don't feed them they don't fight. I don't know about that but I do know that parishes that enjoy sharing food and fellowship are usually happier and more actively involved in a wide variety of ministries than ones where people run out the door right after service. As many people

Altar Guild Chair, Florence Parkins

in the parish would agree, we eat well at Saint John's and we do so because of the commitment of so many people here who cook and share.

A quarter of a century ago there was a wonderful lady named Daisy Caton who seemed to live in the parish kitchen. For many years she was always there cooking and cleaning. Whenever the Rector had a class or meeting he need only tell Ms. Daisy how many people would be there and she would see that everyone was well fed. After she died many others have given their time and talent to the delight of the rest of us, chief among them recently are Daphne Johnson and Margarita Walsh, who provide wonderful food each week after our Saturday Evening Mass.

Nicole Monroe, Parish Almoner

Coffee Hour after Mass and Iced Tea Hour in the Garden during the summer are wonderful times of sharing food providing the opportunity for people to get to know one another. Lately several pews have been removed from the Narthex to facilitate this sort of fellowship even more as we offer wine and refreshment after concerts and other events. On Saturday evenings for the past several years the Contemplative Mass has been followed by a popular Pot Luck Supper. And on the first Sunday of every month many people make a special effort to be at church to share in the community luncheon offered by Saint Margaret's Guild.

But we don't just share food with one another here at Saint John's. As we saw earlier, one of the first committees founded 25 years ago was the Social Concerns Committee, committed to discovering and meeting the needs of those around us. Every week food is brought in to share through the local soup kitchen called CHIPS, Christian Help in Park Slope. Electra Weeks has taken charge of the Turkey Drive each Thanksgiving for many years. She spends hours in the kitchen with other volunteers cooking turkey and all the trimmings to be shared through CHIPS not only for the homeless, but also with the elderly in the community. Other activities through the years have included creating Easter baskets for those in nursing homes, gathering clothing for the homeless and toys for kids at Christmas, serving those with AIDS each Christmas, Easter and Thanksgiving through God's Love We Deliver, and so much more.

Electra Weeks, Thanksgiving Turkey

Bruce Goerlich was the first chair of this committee and others have included Dawn Wheeler, Anna Anderson, Sally Brodsky, Electra Weeks and many others. Today, the committee is part of our Almoner's Guild which is chaired by Nicole Monroe. All donations to the Clergy Discretionary Fund are made available for the relief of those in need through the Social Concerns Committee.

The Rector and vestry discussed Evangelism in 2008 and considered how we might best

Above the new Toddler area in the old chapel.
Below , after the creation of the child friendly space so many new families joined that we needed to baptize ten babies at one service a few months later!

approach congregational growth in Park Slope. One thing we noted was that the neighborhood now included many young families with children. We decided that we would like to become known as a "child friendly" sort of parish. So we asked our Building Chair, Larry Bickford, to remove a few pews and construct a **Toddler Zone.** It contains small chairs and tables with coloring books and other toys as well as rocking chairs and comfortable places for parents to sit. It was an immediate success! Within a few months we had attracted so many young families with children that we had 10 baptisms on June 14 of the next year!

ARTISANS AND BUILDERS

As seen above, one of the key persons in the campaign to **Make Old Things New** was Sally Brodsky. She is an incredibly talented individual who came to Saint John's more than 20 years ago and stayed to share in many aspects of the ministry offered here. One of the ministries she liked doing best was outreach to those in need. For years she led our youth and other volunteers in the New York AIDS Walk, gathered warm clothes and food for the homeless and gifts for poor children at Christmas.

She is also an excellent thurifer, Licensed Eucharistic Minister, and has served with distinction as Warden and Building Committee Chair. In her early adult life Sally was a set designer for opera so she brought her artistic skills with her and we put them to good use. She was married to an architect and had a lot of experience working with contractors, and we made good use of that as well!

Each Christmas we think fondly of her, even though she has retired and moved to upstate New York, as we pull out the worn but beloved parish Nativity figures. Made up of a variety of pieces from different styles and periods it has its own unique charm. But it had fallen on hard times and some were suggesting that we replace it with something

The Holy Family, part of our mismatched Nativity Set

more modern. Sally came to the rescue repainting and repairing each piece. (Except for the donkey, Brian McAnuff painted that and he loved to warn people to *"be careful with my Ass"*.)

After Luke Fodor painted the Chancel a deep blue the damask cloth covering the organ cabinets looked faded and dirty so Sally ordered new deep blue damask and asked Larry Bickford to help her stretch and tack it in place. They made a great team! We all hated to see her retire to a house in the country near Hudson, New York, but Christ Church up there was glad to have her! She immediately joined the staff in their soup kitchen preparing meals each week for those in need.

God was good to us by sending us someone who could take her place caring for the Building and Grounds even before she left us. Larry Bickford, who had worked alongside her brought his own wonderful talents to this holy place. In fact, the floods mentioned above (footnote 37) have been cured at long last (we dearly hope!) due to the hard work he put in installing new pumps and drains.

Larry is a contractor who was born and raised on a farm in north eastern Vermont. He started attending Saint John's about 7 or 8 years ago, shortly after he married his wife, Amethyst. Originally from Nevis, in the West Indies, she was a widow with a young son Larry has lovingly raised as his own. An Anglican from birth, Amethyst encouraged Larry to attend church with her and he did, somewhat quietly at first. After a few months he joined a Bible study class and later joined the Book Club and Confirmation Class. During all this time he was constantly repairing things

Church Wardens and Building Committee Chairpersons
Larry Bickford and Sally Brodsy

around the church and became Building Chair when elected to vestry. He has continued in that post as Church Warden. Without any doubt whatsoever, we could not have accomplished the repairs and renovations done in the past two years without the dedication of time and talent of both of these wonderful people.

Just weeks before this book was printed the final repairs to the exterior and interior of the church building due to the tornado damage mentioned earlier were completed. That tornado was a tragic disaster for us, but like so many other disasters it had a bit of a silver lining. The church had not been painted in about 60 years and the plaster and paint inside were becoming a quite shabby. The seven beautiful lancet windows in the Chapel installed in 1965 were still lovely but their exterior wooden frames were badly deteriorated. So, while the

The wings of the angel in our Memorial Garden were broken by the winds of a tornado. It now sits on a stone removed from the bellcote. The angel was almost thrown out and the stone was rejected because it was old and worn. Repaired and joined together, they are more beautiful than either was before. A wonderful symbol of the new life that God offers to everyone in the Church,

scaffolding was in place they were repaired, a new cross topped the repaired bellcote replacing the one lost so many years before, and the interior of the church got a wonderful face-lift with new plaster and paint!

The Chancel area was painted in deep blue colors several years before to correspond with the descriptions of the blue and gold decoration of the building as it was described in the *Brooklyn Daily Eagle* at its opening service. This created a much more dramatic framing of the worship area and now the Nave, which was a pale green, is a light shade of blue so that it all ties together nicely.

Taking the old stone down and installing the new stones as the interior is plastered and painted.

On June 10, 2012 we celebrated the completion of all the work on the building and our 186th Anniversary with a wonderful service of Solemn Evensong followed by a fantastic garden party. In an article submitted to the Dominion, our Diocesan Newspaper and to the Brooklyn Daily Eagle newspaper, our Parish Administrator, James Olszewski described it this way:

The scene on St. John's Place in the Park Slope section of Brooklyn on the evening of Sunday, June 10 was one of pure jubilation. The congregation of St. John's gathered with neighbors from the surrounding community to celebrate the parish's 186th Anniversary. The festivities began with a traditional service of Evensong featuring a refined selection of music, brilliantly and prayerfully delivered by the St. John's Choir under the direction of Cryder H. Bankes III. One of these selections was a beautiful version of the Magnificat composed by St. John's own Beth Anderson-Harold which was first unveiled last year at the Evensong celebrating the parish's 185th Anniversary. The service also provided an ample opportunity for a homecoming as The Rev. Luke Fodor, Curate of St. John's Church, Cold Spring Harbor came back to preach at the church that sponsored him for theological study. His thoughtful words added to the joyous sentiment of the day.

Following the service, the celebration continued with a Garden Party just outside the church. There was a plenty to eat thanks to Electra Weeks and company who provided a fantastic spread. There was plenty to drink, including a special cocktail whipped together for this special occasion by Doug Hecklinger. You could hear the sounds of people mingling with those they had seen recently, not for awhile or had never met before, but the best sounds were coming from Bob Mackie and the band. The Rector of St. John's, Father Clark Powers heard from a great many of attendees that it was a fantastic event and he concurred, "I have to agree that it was a fantastic afternoon that we will never forget! That is what an anniversary celebration should be about - remembering where we came from and creating new memories to cherish in future years."

At this anniversary, the people of St. John's Church have plenty to be excited about. Just weeks before, a massive restoration project that had the church shackled with scaffolding and draped in darkness for months, came to an end. In fact, this was the first time some people were inside the church to see the newly painted interior and the first opportunity to use the entire garden since the work began.

If you could have seen this event celebrating 186 years of worship and service at St. John's firsthand, you would find it impossible to imagine this parish not still thriving 186 years from now!

I could not agree more! Below are some pictures of that celebration.

With the new stonework, the plaster and paint inside, the relatively new kitchen and gardens and, above all, with the faith and commitment of our people, Saint John's Church is ready to begin another chapter of Our Story.

At the end of his Gospel Saint John said,

But there are also many other things which Jesus did; were every one of them to be written, I suppose that the world itself could not contain the books that would be written.

And there are many other things that have happened here in this holy place which are not mentioned in this brief history. Laughter and tears have been shared in this place as God has been worshipped and God's people have been served. So many people have come and gone and left their mark of love and sacrifice that have combined to make this place special and holy. May God bless them and those who are yet to come and witness here to God's love.

In our first parish register Father Evan Malbone Johnson, our first and founding rector, wrote:

In consequence of the increasing growth of the Village of Brooklyn, the design of building a new Episcopal Church was formed by Evan Malbone Johnson in the Spring of A.D. 1826. In the course of that summer, he caused a plain wooden building to be erected at the corner of Washington and Johnson Streets, said building is fifty feet by fifty. It was first opened by him for divine Service on <u>Sunday the 26th of September 1826</u>. The communion was first administered on Easter Day A.D. (<u>April 15, 1827</u>) to nineteen communicants. The Church was consecrated by the Right Rev. Bishop Hobart on the <u>10th</u>

of July (1827) and called Saint John's Church. May God bless "his handy work".

Evan M. Johnson, 1827

It is appropriate to end this edition of the history of this parish with those words inscribed with so much faith and hope as that history began. May God continue to bless ***"his handy work."***

Clarence H. Powers, 2012

Father Powers,
16th Rector
Saint John's Church

The Narthex Art Show, part of our 186th Anniversary, June 13, 2012

Our Vestry

The current members of Saint John's Vestry are reflective of the congregation they represent. Members include a Contractor, a Doctor of Psychiatry, a University Professor, an Elementary School Teacher, a Graphic Artist, two Social Workers, an Office Administrator, a Nutritionist, a House Wife, a College Student. They are black and white, young and not so young, male and female, gay and straight, and all committed to the ministry of Christ in this place.

Officers

Church Warden Larry Bickford, Treasurer Don Derrick, Church Warden Pat Pegram

Vestry Members
Right to Left: Maria Moyser, William Hunter, Becky Rafter, Florence Parkins, Doug Hecklinger, Elena McCalla , Nicole Monroe, Kimberly Lyons, Juliet Emanuel- George

Rectors of Saint John's

1.	The Reverend Evan Malbone Johnson	1826-1847
2.	The Reverend Samuel Roosevelt Johnson	1847-1850
3.	The Reverend N. A. Okeson	1850 - 1853
4.	The Reverend Thomas F. Guion	1853-1862
5.	The Reverend George F. Seymour	1863-1866
6.	The Reverend Alexander Burgess	1867-1868
7.	The Reverend R. E. Terry	1869-1874
8.	The Reverend T. S. Pycott	1874-1887
9.	The Reverend George F. Breed	1887-1903
10.	The Reverend Frank D. Page	1903-1911
11.	The Reverend Thomas Bond Holland	1911-1930
12.	The Reverend Gordon D. Pierce	1931-1950
13.	The Reverend Howard G. Clark	1950-1956
14.	The Reverend Donald James Gardner	1956-1958
15.	The Reverend Clifford Allen Buck	1958-1985
16.	The Reverend Clarence Powers	1987 –

Parish Anniversary Fund

Sponsors

Contributed $185 or More

The Altar Guild, Saint Margaret's Guild, Suzy Hsia and Steve Adams, Cryder Bankes, Adina Bent, Larry and Amethyst Bickford, Joyce Blake, Jocelyn Bradley, Sally Brodsky, Don Derrick, Juliet Emanuel-George, Shirley Emanuel, Johnson and Omoladun Esho, Luke and Willow Fodor, Wilma Forde, Violet Harper, Roy and Catherine Haynes, Janet Hibbert, Bill and Eris Hunter, Uriah and Gertrude Insular, Fred and Beulah Jacob, Daphne Johnson, Rosemarie Kent, Alan Kramer, Katie Locke, Janet Mackey, Susan McHenry, Nicole Monroe, John and Patty Pegram, Cheryl Plambeck and Brian Hayes, Father Clark Powers, John Villios, Daphne Watson, Eunice Watkins, Kathryn Cullen-DuPont, Sherry Weaver-Chetrit, Celia and Armando Jones, Veda Perry, Patrick Cheek

Patrons

Contributed $92.50 or More

Humberto and Marilyn Arjonilla, Florence Baird, Victoria Hill, Fred and Beulah Jacob, John and Barbara Muir, Charmaine Jacob, Gweneth Marcelli, Maria Moyser, Barbara Stewart, Paul Chetrit, Margarita Walsh, J.M. Walsh,

Contributors

Raymond DeVera, Milcah McQueen, Sheila Reid, Carolyn Stallworth, Rosslyn Wickham. Milcah McQueen, Sharon Nicholson Roderique, Esther Arrington, Phillip Braithwaite, John Guidry, Terrie Collymore, Grace Bond, Nate Green, Hilda Coleman, Eleonor Yard, Grace Garnett

End Notes

Listed below are three things I am calling End Notes. Referenced in the text, they are far too long to be inserted as footnotes, but are of significant value to understanding the history of the parish. The first of these includes the entire sermon delivered by the first Rector of the parish who was invited to speak at the re-opening of the newly decorated wooden building in 1861. In his sermon he delivered an invaluable summary of his 20 years of ministry in the parish.

The second note below is a listing of the amazing number of Episcopal Churches founded in the shot span of time between 1795 - 1869 here in Brooklyn. If you are reading this in an e-book you will have live links to take you online to their own stories.

The last note below is really part of the third note in that it is that portion of the online history of the Episcopal Church in Brooklyn having to do with Saint John's Church. It is quite a nice little summary of our history and we will probably make use of it in constructing a small pamphlet of our history to make available to visitors.

I *Publication: Brooklyn Eagle; Date: Oct 14, 1861; Section: None; Page Number:2*

Reopening of Saint Johns Church — Reminiscences of Old Brooklyn

The old *"Church in the Meadows"* endeared to us by so many pleasant associations and regretful memories was re-opened yesterday by the memorable Bishop Potter, in the presence of a full congregation. Just before the sermon, the Pastor, Mr. Guion, in brief and appropriate words, welcomed his parishioners back to, their old homestead, and commended their liberality In the reconstruction of the good old Church, which had been effected without any great burden of debt. Bishop Potter, on taking the pulpit, congratulated the congregation and its beloved pastor on the consummation of their labors, and delivered a most impressive discourse. At evening services, the Reverend E.M. Johnson spoke in eloquent words of the old times before us. The historical portion of the Domine's sermon is all we can find room for:

Twenty three years ago, after having, been admitted to orders about a year before, your preacher came to reside upon this island. Saint James' Church, New York was the scene of his labors for twelve years. Private business calling him frequently to visit Brooklyn, he became convinced that the growth of this place would soon warrant the erection of a second Episcopal Church in the spring of 1828, he caused a church to be built at an expense of $3,600, on this spot. At the laying of the corner stone, it was called Saint John's, which name was determined upon by lot. This was done without any previous, conference with any of the inhabitants, for fear of exciting the jealousy of the members of the old church.

The church, and most of you saw it before its' first enlargement, was opened by your preacher on the 24th of September, 1826 the first time for divine service. The services of the Reverend J. Hicks were procured, and during the fall and winter the pulpit was alternately supplied by him and myself. I do not think the number of families who attended was more than eight or ten, individually from twenty to thirty. In the spring of '27, I removed with my family to Brooklyn, and resigned the charge which I had so long held and left New York, and with it a salary that had hitherto, from necessity, been my chief support. The communion was first administered to nineteen communicants at Easter,'27, of whom six are now of our number—two only having died—and the rest, have removed away or left us.

The first election of wardens and vestrymen was held on Easter Monday, '27; of those who were elected, one warden and three vestrymen are at present members, and have continued to belong to this corporation. One of the first efforts made to enlarge the usefulness of this church was the establishment of the Sunday school in this neighborhood. It began to be thickly settled, and by a class of people whose children much needed instruction. A few were found who volunteered their aid, and a Sunday School for children was then established.

The year after its establishment the school house was built by subscription at an expense of $600. Since then there has been at different , times connected with this school 77 teachers and 909 children; the present number of conductors is 21, and of children 272. Many of those who have been teachers, and some who have been scholars are now settled in life—some heads of families and members of this congregation. One is in the University, another a candidate for the same and two others having that in view.

A valuable library, which I wish were larger than it is, belongs to the school, consisting of 400 volumes. This School has been supported by collections and subscriptions; the whole amount for the school and for the library is about $800, an amount of money well laid out yielding an usurious interest. In the year 1831, (through the, instrumentality of my late lamented wife) the ladies of the congregation formed a Benevolent Society. This Society has held its regular' meetings and an annual fair. It has been instrumental in promoting a spirit of active benevolence among those who are disposed to the exercise of this Christian grace. It has enabled its members to extend aid to the distressed, and has afforded succor to many, very many, needy individuals. It has for the last two years consisted of 92 members, and during its existence has distributed $1,500 in various acts of charity and mercy. It has been doubly useful to those who have contributed and to those who have received of its funds. During each year since its existence collections have been made for various objects connected with our missionary establishments: our Bible Society, the Colonization Society and Tract Society. In June, 1833, a Missionary Association was formed in the congregation. Since that time there has been collected for various objects the sum of $842, and it is believed a sum not much short of that had been previously collected, making in all about $1,500 for these commendable objects. In the spring of 1832 it was determined by the vestry to enlarge and beautify this temple of the Lord—the building, originally 50 feet square, was extended to its present length, 85 feet, the tower built, and the church as we now see it; a bell and organ procured. This was done at an expense of about $8,000- $4,000 of which was generously advanced by Trinity Church, upon condition that at the expiration of ten years the church should be placed out of debt. The debt of the church is now $5,000, being its original coat together with the, ground on which it stands. The only method to pay it is from the sale of pews, the weekly collections, and the saving of its pew rents during the incumbency of its present Rector. I would at this time most respectfully urge upon this congregation the importance of extinguishing this as soon as possible, while the demands upon the funds are comparatively small. The future permanency of the church calls for this measure, and there is abundant ability with the members of the congregation to effect this object at once if they so determine. There have been, united in holy matrimony by the minister of this church since its organization, 215 couples. There has been baptized: adults, 31; children, 427; in all 458. There has been 4 confirmations, in the church, of which 114 persons have received that holy rite.

Baptisms

1826 to 1837	458
1837-1847	888
Total	1346

Marriages

1826-1837	215
1837 -1847	372
Total	587

Communicants

1827-1837	213	
1837-1847	286	
Total	499	

There are now 125 communicants belonging here and have been since we commenced, 213 in all; some have died and others removed. I have not the means of ascertaining the precise number of families who consider themselves belonging to this congregation, for many do not either own or hire pews; and as long as we have vacant room so ought we to be glad to accommodate such. I should think as many have belonged here and have removed away as now compose the congregation. Thus much has been accomplished in ten years. This vine planted in dependence on the rains and dews of God's providence has continued to grow and flourish. The Lord has built up this house - He has blessed the means, and to Him be all the praise. It is of course a source of gratification, to your preacher that this (as was deemed by many) experiment has succeeded. He has already abundantly been rewarded for all his exertions. He has received his reward in that which it far better than any worldly consideration—the approbation of his own conscience and the belief, that he has in some small degree been of service to the souls of many of his fellow creatures. Though there has been at no one time any great or sudden revival among us, yet there has been a gradual advance and growth in piety and grace; he has indeed cause to mourn that many, many have sat under his ministry and seem to be where they were. Yet he cannot see the heart; of one thing we may indeed be thankful- we have enjoyed a great degree of peace and union. No disputes or jars have at any time disturbed our quiet intercourse, and perhaps in few congregations are the families which compose it more in the habit of social intercourse. It has hitherto been necessary for me to devote more attention to the secular affairs of the church than I will be able to do for the future. I shall expect hereafter that those measures which we find to be necessary for the outward establishment of this church shall be the special care of its vestry. The payment of the debt; the securing of more ground around, the sale of remaining pews; (provision for the support of its assistant minister)—these are all intimately connected with the permanent building up of this Lord's house. To you brethren of the vestry and congregation the care of these things is committed, and I am well persuaded you will attend to them and put this chinch upon so stable a foundation that it will continue to be a blessing to your children's children. It remains for me to consider our text in a higher and spiritual sense. Unless there be here an increase and growth in grace; unless the standard of moral virtue be high; unless we find the ordinances of preaching the sacraments are here the means of making us better and fitting us more and more for eternal bliss—unless, I say, there things be so we cannot say, the Lord prospers this work. It is one thing for a congregation to grow in numbers and in its outward state, another for its members to grow in the graces of the spirit. While then each one who belongs to us strives to do good to this Zion, to advance its outward interest, let everyone also strive by his own example, and by increasing knowledge and virtue, to make ours to be a city set on a hill. Let us be thankful to God for the good which may hitherto have been effected, and remember that to relax our exertions in His cause or service is to betray our trust. To you, my hearers, who are heads of families and have children, I say, let your desire and exertions be to establish firmly this house of God, as a means of affording to posterity the opportunity of His worship. What you leave them invested in the treasury of the Lord will not be the least valuable of their inheritance. Finally, my dear brethren, you who have here taken in full the Saviour's name, much depends on you. "Let your light so shine before men, that they may see your good works, and see your Father which is in heaven." We have a right to expect your best exertions and your warmest prayers for this Zion where you placed your names. May you be enabled, by your walk and conversation to recommend others the way you have chosen. May the opportunities for spiritual communion which you here enjoy be faithfully improved, so that at last we may all gather around our Father's board in that kingdom where there shall be no more need of outward tabernacles or carnal ordinances.

II Brooklyn Episcopal Parishes Established from 1795 - 1869

1. St. Ann's founded 1795
2. St. John's founded 1826
3. St. Paul's founded 1833
4. Trinity founded 1835
5. Christ Church founded 1837
6. Church of Our Savior founded 1860
7. Christ Church Red Hook Mission
8. St. Mary's founded 1840
9. Emmanuel Church founded 1841
10. Calvary Free Church founded 1840
11. St. Luke's Church founded 1842
12. St. Thomas's Church founded 1844
13. The Church of the Holy Trinity founded 1844
14. Grace Church founded 1847
15. Protestant Episcopal Church of the Reformation 1847
16. St. Michael's Church founded 1847
17. St. Peter's founded 1847
18. St. Paul's Church, Clinton and Carroll sts. founded 1849
19. St. Mark's Church founded 1850
20. The Church of the Messiah founded 1850
21. St. George's Church founded 1852
22. Church of the Redeemer founded 1853
23. Emmanuel Church founded 1853
24. Christ Church Mission Chapel founded 1857
25. The Free Church St. Matthew's founded 1859
26. The Church of the Reformation founded 1866
27. St. Thomas (now Guion Church) founded 1868
28. St. Andrew's Church founded 1859
29. Church of the Atonement founded 1864
30. The Church of Our Savior founded 1867
31. The Church of the Evangelists founded 1867
32. Chapel of the Holy Trinity Church founded 1867
33. St. James's Church founded 1868
34. St. Stephen's Chapel founded 1869
35. All Saints Chapel founded 1867
36. Church of the Mediator founded 1869

37. St. Mark's Church, E.D. founded 1837
38. Christ Church, E.D. founded 1846
39. St. Paul's, E.D. founded 1846
40. St. James's Church, E.D. founded 1846
41. Calvary (Free) Church, E.D. founded 1849
42. Church of the Ascension, Greenpoint founded 1846
43. St. John's Church, E.D. founded 1851
44. Ascension Church, Bushwick, E.D. founded 1852
45. Grace Church, E.D. founded 1853
46. St. Barnabas Chapel, E.D. founded 1851

III History of Episcopal Churches in Brooklyn
Saint John's Church from
http://www.panix.com/~cassidy/STILES/EPISCOPALCHURCHES.html)

St. John's Church, on the corner of Washington and Johnson streets, was erected during the summer of 1826. This parish owes its origin and maintenance during many of its earlier years, to the foresight and liberality of its first rector, the Rev. Evan M. Johnson. [40] The edifice, built by the Rev. Mr.

---

[40]*Rev. Evan M. Johnson, was born June 6, 1792, at Newport, R. I., to which place his Quaker ancestors had been driven by the religious intolerance of Massachusetts colony where they first settled. His mother was of a Virginia family. After obtaining a classical education, he passed one year at college, in Rhode Island, and two years at Cambridge, Mass., where he became a candidate for orders, and received ordination at Trinity church, Newport, from the hands of Bishop Griswold, July 8, 1813. Residing, after his ordination, with his mother at Plainfield, Conn.. he was invited to preach for a short time at Norwalk, Conn., and while there accidentally met the Rev. Dr. Bowen, Rector of Grace church, Now York, who shortly after invited him to come to that city as his curate. A year of service at Grace church was terminated by a can from the Episcopal church at Newtown, L. I., where he went in 1814, and remained until 1826. In 1814, lie married Maria L., daughter of John B. Johnson, of New York, by whom he had one son, still living. This lady dying in 1825, be soon afterwards married Maria Purdy, of Newtown, L. I., by whom lie had three children. By his first marriage lie became associated with the interests of the large estate of his father-in-law, which was left by will to his children. While at Newtown, he owned and managed a farm, which lie endeavored for a time to sell, with out finding a purchaser. He then resolved that, if lie could sell his farm for*

Johnson at his own expense, on his own land, and for several years gener- ously furnished to the congregation free of cost, was first opened for divine service on the 24th of September, 1826 ; and for a few months be was assisted in the services by the Rev. John A. Hicks. On Easter day, 1827, there were nineteen communicants. [41]

$4,000 he would devote that sum to the building of a church. An opportunity of sale won after occurring, he left his church in Newtown, in 1826, much to the regret of his parishioners, and removed to Brooklyn, N. Y., where he erected St. John's church. His personal history thenceforth, to the day of his death, is inseparably interwoven with the spiritual and material interests of the city of Brooklyn. In addition to building St. John's, he undertook the establishment, in 1847, of St. Michael's amid a crowded and neglected population, and 11 it was his peculiar and honorable record, that for services in that church and all other churches, for forty years of his ministry, he never received a cent of remuneration. And this not because he was rich. The property which came to his care, had to be improved by building and other loans, which required large realizations to pay the interest, and nothing but great attention and I good management could have kept it from becoming submerged by taxes and assessments, in the advancing progress of Brooklyn.

In his plans for improving his property, he went extensively into improvements embracing in their scope the map of the whole city. Nothing of Brooklyn was without interest to him; its City Hall, its parks, its ferries, its streets. To his exertions was owing the opening of that great eastern wing of the city, Myrtle avenue. This, though now a closely built thoroughfare, was carried through entirely by the perseverance of our subject. On the petition asking for it was his single name, against four hundred remonstrants, and yet it was achieved, and the lots thereon have been brought into use and quadrupled In value. In effecting this he was aided by Jonathan Trotter, mayor, and Gabriel Furman, alderman of the first ward." Mr. Johnson's good nature and liberal tendencies caused him to be, extensively sought by parties desirous of being united in matrimony, and at the time of his half century discourse, the number of marriages performed by him had reached as high as two thousand. No man's life was more studded with deeds of actual and daily kindness than the domine's, as he was generally called throughout the city. He would at any time rise at midnight or daylight to marry the humblest couple or do the smallest deed of kindness. During the whole of his life here, none of our clergymen was ever half so much seen among the people as the domine. Almost any day at about ten or eleven o'clock he might be seen turning the corner of Pearl street from the north Into Myrtle avenue; for he lived where his ancient farm house stood, and in walking through Pearl street follows in some degree the ancient cowpath of his farm. His style of drew was plain, simple and old fashioned, a felt hat, always carelessly crumpled ground the rim, surmounted the face of an ancient Roman, crowned with a strong crop of standing hair, as white as snow; and an atmosphere of ease and benignity surrounded him, inviting everybody to stop and have a chat with him. He might have been, and indeed frequently was, taken for one of the ancient crop of Dutchmen, an error which his name assisted in producing ; but, as we have seen, the nearest he came to it was in marrying into a Dutch family.

[41] *The church was named by lot, at the time of laying the corner-stone, - which was done," says Mr. Johnson's manuscripts, " without any Previous conference with any of*

The day following, Theodosius Hunt and William Furman were elected church-wardens, and Evan Malbone, Joseph N. Smith, William A. Sale, Henry Dikeman, Isaac Odell, Gabriel Furman, John Taylor, and Nathan B. Morse, vestrymen. On the 10th of July, of the same year, the church was consecrated by Bishop Hobart. The attendance continuing to increase, it was considerably enlarged and improved in 1832, and purchased by the congregation. In 1835, the Rev. Jacob W. Diller became assistant minister; and in 1841, the Rev. Stephen Patterson officiated in the same relation for a year, and was followed by the Rev. Caleb S. Henry, D.D., Professor of Moral Philosophy in the University of the City of New York. A few years later, still further quite extensive repairs and improvements were made in the church especially in the arrangements of the chancel. In July, 1847, the Rev. Mr. Johnson withdrew, after the long period of over twenty years of faithful services, without remuneration; in order to establish a free mission church, St. Michael's. in a neighborhood destitute of all church privileges, where he gratuitously and successfully labored for the remainder of his days. He was succeeded in St. John's by the Rev, Samuel R. Johnson, D.D., also a devoted pastor and liberal benefactor of the parish; who, however, resigned on the 18th of November, 1850, having been elected Professor of Systematic Divinity in the General Theological Seminary in New York.

The Rev. N. A. Okeson, D.D., next filled the rectorship, entering upon his duties on the first of January, 1851, and witnessed a considerable increase in the numbers and strength of the congregation, but removed in October, 1852, and became the pastor of St. Paul's church, Norfolk, Va. His successor was the Rev. Thomas T. Guion, D.D., who commenced his labors on the 1st of February, 1853, and remained in charge until his death, in the autumn of 1862. At the end of two years, by a judicious arrangement of systematic offerings, the debt was entirely extinguished. Six years afterwards, in 1861, "a plan was resolved upon for a renovation" of the church, so extensive as to amount almost to a re- edification of the decayed and unsightly structure. He lived to see that plan fulfilled, together with the erection of a new chapel, at a total cost of about twelve thousand dollars. For a few weeks only was he permitted to minister in this beautified sanctuary, when unexpectedly he was smitten down." He was buried from the church on the 24th of October, 1862, amid a large concourse of the clergy, and of his parishioners and friends.

For a few months, until permanent arrangements could be made, the Rev. George W. Nichols took charge of the services, aided by the Rev. Henry A. Spafard,

---

the inhabitants, for fear of exciting the jealousy of the members of the old (Reformed Dutch) church."

before and since an assistant minister of the parish. In June, 1863, the Rev. George F. Seymour, D.D., accepted a call to the vacant rectorate, visiting the church once a month to administer the holy communion, until the first of October, when he removed to Brooklyn and took charge. Called to the Chair of Ecclesiastical History in the General Seminary in 1865, he terminated his connection with the parish on the feast of Epiphany, 1867, when the Rev. Alexander Burgess, D.D., assumed charge.

From 1826 to January, 1868, there were two thousand four hundred and thirty-one baptisms, nine hundred and twenty-seven marriages, and one thousand seven hundred and ninety-nine communicants; four hundred and eighteen being at present connected with the parish. A rectory has of late been enlarged and fitted up, adjoining the church.

In 1868, the old building, corner of Washington and Johnson streets, was sold for $90,000; and the corner-stone of a new chapel was laid, at the corner of Seventh and Douglass streets, on the 15th of June, 1869. This chapel is of red sandstone, and will accommodate about four hundred persons; a new rectory adjoins the chapel of the same material, the cost of both being about $40,000.

Read More at

http://www.panix.com/~cassidy/STILES/EPISCOPALCHURCHES.html

MAPS AND ILLUSTRATIONS

Index

Made in the USA
Charleston, SC
26 May 2013